Fascinating Facts for Curious Minds

Amazing Facts, Games, and Quizzes about the Universe, Dinosaurs, Technology, Flowers, Animals, Scientists and More

By

Eli Spark

Table of Content

Introduction

Welcome to a world bursting with fascinating facts and incredible stories! This volume is your passport to exploring the universe's enigmas, the beauty of the natural world, and the extraordinary events of the past. But what is the cause of that curiosity in you? In your case, however, curiosity is a superpower waiting to be unleashed. It makes you wonder, "Why do the stars sparkle in the sky?" What enables certain species of animals to thrive in locations with extreme weather?" Every time you wonder about something, you're using your natural curiosity to learn and grow. Being curious isn't just about asking questions; it's about opening doors to new adventures.

Every single piece of information provided in this volume serves as a gateway to a different universe whether it is on outer space or the incredible animal species found in the world. Such a beginning of telling these facts enables one to benefit from the integrative dynamics of all surroundings. And the more knowledge you gain in such a pursuit, the more it will whet your appetite for further learning. This book is here to help you harness that curiosity and turn it into an exciting journey of discovery.

How to Use This Book

Think of this book as a treasure map, guiding you through different islands of knowledge. Every chapter explores a new subject the secrets of the cosmos to the astonishing abilities of various species. You don't have to read it linearly; feel free to indulge in any chapter that you find appealing. Do you have an interest in dinosaurs, perhaps? Flip right to that chapter and dive in. Want to learn about how technology is changing our world? There's a chapter for that too!

As you explore each chapter, you'll find fun facts, surprising stories, and even quizzes to challenge your newfound knowledge. It's not enough to just read the pages of this book—one has to also think. Why not present these facts to your relations? Perhaps they will learn something surprising for them? This book may also be helpful in some arts and crafts. Maybe you'll find inspiration to draw a picture, write a story, or even invent your own game based on what you learn. The possibilities are endless!

How This Book Can Help with Brain Development

This book isn't just fun; it's also a great workout for your brain. In numerous ways, acquiring novel information acts as a workout for your mind. Every time you learn something new, your brain develops neural pathways that aid in the enhancement of your recalling ability and critical thinking abilities. For instance, when expanding your horizon out into the boundless sky or understanding the behaviors of various species, knowledge of such exotic concepts facilitates the creativity of the individual. It encourages you to ask "What if?" and "How?"—questions that are at the heart of learning and creativity. By diving into a variety of topics, you're also training your brain to be flexible and adaptable. It is recommended to explore various points of view and appreciate the variety and intricacies of the world. Knowledge is one of many skills that increases exponentially the more it is practiced and utilized.

The brain turns into a huge super muscle waiting to be expanded even more with knowledge. And why not? One day, you might use this knowledge to solve real-world problems or make discoveries of your own.So, are you ready to start this adventure? Grab this book and let your curiosity lead the way. Whether it is the sky with its countless stars, the unexplored depths of the sea, or the most fascinating of innovations, keep in mind that every little piece of information helps one learn more about the context (the world) and oneself. That being said, let us flip the page and go straight into the marvels that are in store for us. Your journey of exploration and brain-building starts here!

Chapter 1:
Mysteries of the Universe

The vastness of the cosmos contains fascinating and questionable sights and occurrences such as planets, stars, and even outer space-related phenomena. This section will explore the solar system, making known the planet and the incredible facts beyond all. Get ready to explore the universe's most astonishing secrets!

Wonders of the Solar System

1. **Saturn's Floating Trick**: Saturn is so light for its size that it could float in water—if you could find a bathtub big enough! This is because Saturn is mostly made of gases, and its density is lower than water.

2. **Mercury's Crazy Temperature Swings**: On Mercury, the temperature can go from cold to scorching hot in one day! During the daytime, it can reach 800°F, but at night, it drops to -290°F. It's like going from a sauna to a freezer in just a few hours!

3. **Venus Spins Backward**: Venus is the oddball of the solar system because it spins in the opposite direction to most other planets. If you were standing on Venus, the Sun would rise in the west and set in the east. Talk about confusing!

4. **Neptune's Mysterious Glow**: Neptune gives off more heat than it gets from the Sun, making scientists wonder what's going on inside! This mysterious glow may be due to its shrinking size over time, which could be releasing extra heat from deep within the planet.

5. **The Moon's Quakes**: Did you know that the Moon has "moonquakes"? Unlike Earth's quakes caused by tectonic plates, moonquakes are triggered by the Moon's stretching and shrinking as it orbits the Earth. They can last up to an hour, much longer than most earthquakes!

6. **Pluto's Ice Volcanoes**: Even though Pluto is no longer classified as a planet, it still has some cool features. Scientists discovered that Pluto might have ice volcanoes that spew icy water instead of lava. Imagine frozen geysers erupting from the surface of a dwarf planet!

7. **Uranus Rolls Like a Ball**: Uranus is unique because it spins on its side! Unlike most planets that rotate upright, Uranus rolls like a ball around the Sun, making its poles take turns facing the star. One-half of the planet is in constant sunlight for 42 years at a time!

8. **Earth's "Second" Moon**: Besides the Moon, Earth has another small object called 3753 Cruithne, which some people call Earth's "second moon." It doesn't orbit Earth exactly, but it follows a synchronized path around the Sun, always staying close to our planet.

Fun Fact Quiz

What strange natural phenomenon happens on the Moon that's similar to earthquakes on Earth?

A. Moon storms

B. Moonquakes

C. Moon eruptions

D. Moon lightning

Mysterious Phenomena in Space

1. **The Wow! Signal**: In 1977, scientists picked up a strange radio signal from space that lasted 72 seconds. They named it the "Wow! Signal" because it was so mysterious, and to this day, no one knows where it came from or what caused it!

2. **The Great Attractor**: Deep in space, there's an invisible force called the Great Attractor pulling galaxies (including ours!) towards it. Scientists aren't sure what it is or why it's so powerful, but it's one of the greatest cosmic mysteries.

3. **The Dark Flow**: Scientists have found a strange movement of galaxies called the "Dark Flow." These galaxies seem to be pulled toward something outside the visible universe, but no one knows what it is!

4. **Rogue Planets**: Planets are drifting through space all by themselves, known as "rogue planets." These planets do not have any orbits, making them lonely wanderers in the universe.

5. **The Cold Spot**: There's a giant, unusually cold area in space called the "Cold Spot." Some scientists think it might be evidence of another universe colliding with ours, but no one can say for sure!

6. **The Cosmic Web**: The universe is connected by a network of filaments called the Cosmic Web. These are made of dark

matter and gas, stretching across the universe and linking galaxies together like a giant spider web.

7. **Zombie Stars**: Sometimes, stars that have exploded in a supernova can come back to life! These "zombie stars" re-ignite and flare up again, making scientists scratch their heads and wonder how it happens.

Fun Fact Quiz

What might the Cold Spot in space be evidence of?

A. A massive black hole

B. A distant galaxy

C. Another universe

D. A comet passing by

Our Wonderful Planet

1. **There's a Place on Earth Where It Never Rains**: The Atacama Desert in Chile does not come to terms with water and humidity. Some weather stations in this desert have never recorded a single drop of rain, making it almost like a Martian landscape!

2. **We're Spinning Fast**: Earth rotates at about 1,000 miles per hour, so we're all spinning around fast even though we don't feel it! This rapid rotation is what makes our days 24 hours long.

3. **The Earth Has Two Types of Crust**: The outermost layer of the Earth, referred to as the crust, is comprised of two principal types; the continental crust, which constitutes the land mass, and the oceanic crust which is found under the water bodies. The oceanic crust is thinner but denser than the continental crust.

4. **Antarctica Is the Largest Desert on Earth**: Even though it's covered in ice, Antarctica is the biggest desert on planet earth! It's classified as a desert because it gets very little rainfall—less than 2 inches of rain every year. That makes it even drier than the Sahara Desert!

5. **Earth's Atmosphere Protects Us from Space**: Our planet's atmosphere acts like a shield, protecting us from harmful Sun radiation and space radiation. It also keeps meteors from crashing into Earth by burning them up as they enter!

6. **Earth Has a Gold Layer Deep Inside**: Deep beneath the Earth's surface, there's enough gold to cover the planet in a 1.5-foot-thick layer! Most of it is located near the core, so it's too far down to reach, but it's still an amazing fact!

Fun Fact Quiz

What is the biggest desert on Planet Earth?

A. Sahara Desert

B. Gobi Desert

C. Arabian Desert

D. Antarctica

The Search for Extraterrestrial Life

1. **The Drake Equation**: To gauge the number of extraterrestrial civilizations that may exist in the Milky Way galaxy, scientists deploy the computation referred to as the Drake's equation. While it doesn't give a definite answer, it helps us imagine how many planets out there could have life!

2. **Mars Might Have Had Life**: Mars was once much warmer and wetter, making scientists think it could have supported life billions of years ago. NASA's rovers are still looking for clues, like fossils or signs of ancient microbes, to see if Mars ever had living creatures.

3. **SETI: The Alien Listening Program**: SETI (Search for Extraterrestrial Intelligence) is a program that listens for signals from space. It uses giant radio telescopes to scan the sky in the hope of hearing messages from intelligent alien civilizations.

4. **Alien Life Could Be Microbial**: When we think of aliens, we often imagine little green men, but scientists think that if life exists on other planets, it might be tiny microbes or bacteria—like the earliest forms of life on Earth.

5. **The Fermi Paradox**: The Fermi Paradox asks a simple question: if the universe is so big, and there are so many stars and planets, why haven't we found any aliens yet? Scientists have many theories, but the answer is still a mystery.

6. **UFOs: Unidentified Flying Objects**: Over the years, people have reported seeing strange objects in the sky, which some believe are UFOs sent by aliens. While most of these sightings have been explained, some remain mysterious and fuel our curiosity about extraterrestrial life.

7. **Life on Venus?** Scientists recently discovered traces of a gas called phosphine in Venus's clouds. On Earth, phosphine is usually made by living organisms, which makes some researchers wonder if there could be life floating in Venus's atmosphere.

8. **Could We Be the Aliens?** Some scientists believe in the "Panspermia" theory, which suggests that life on Earth might

have come from somewhere else in space, like a comet or asteroid. If that's true, we could all be "aliens" ourselves!

Fun Fact Quiz

Which planet in our solar system might have had life billions of years ago?

A. Venus

B. Mars

C. Neptune

D. Jupiter

Game
Planet Match-Up

Greetings, intergalactic traveler! After acquiring knowledge concerning the Tips Geocycling Activities and the rest of the universe, engaging in a worthwhile activity is important. Can you assist in associating these topics with the special descriptions of the planets?

How to Play:

Step 1: Using a blank sheet of paper, jot down the titles of all the planets in our solar system like Mercury, Venus, Earth, Mars and others.

Step 2: Write also below the names of some interesting descriptions of the planets (for example: "This planet is very hot!" or "This one has rings!").

Step 3: Then connect the description with the name of the planet you think best corresponds to the description with a line.

Tip: What did you just learn, think about it—which information is interesting and fun, what did you use from the chapter? When you do all this, you become a Planet Pro!

Chapter 2:
Wild and Wacky Animals

Get ready to immerse yourself in the animal kingdom, where creatures have superpowers that seem straight out of a superhero movie! To be able to survive in their respective environments, animals have developed some of the most astounding powers over the years. In this chapter, you will come across animals that can change color, squirt water, and even punch like a boxer! Such interesting forms of evolution are exciting because they help us appreciate nature and the ingenuity of animals in asking for survival even in the strangest ways. So, buckle up and prepare to be amazed by the unbelievable skills and tricks of the animal kingdom!

Unbelievable Animal Superpowers

1. **Cheetahs Are Speed Machines**: Cheetahs can sprint at speeds of up to 70 miles per hour! This makes them the fastest land animals on Earth. However, they can only keep this incredible speed for about 20-30 seconds before needing to rest.

2. **Electric Eels Can Zap Their Prey**: Electric eels have electric power to generate a shock of 600 volts! They use this electric power to defend themselves and to catch prey. That's enough electricity to knock out a human or power several light bulbs.

3. **Frogs Can Freeze Without Dying**: Some frogs have the amazing ability to survive being frozen solid! When temperatures drop, wood frogs can stop their hearts and freeze their bodies, only to thaw out and hop away when the weather warms up.

4. **Dung Beetles Are Super Strong**: Dung beetles are the strongest animals in the world relative to their size. They can lift objects more than 1000 times that of their body weight. To put it into perspective, this would be like a person carrying no less than 6 double-decker buses.

5. **Pistol Shrimp's Sonic Snap**: The pistol shrimp has one of the most powerful snaps in the ocean! It snaps its claw so fast that it creates a bubble, which bursts with such force that it stuns prey and even produces a tiny flash of light. Talk about a super-powered snap!

6. **Tardigrades Can Survive Almost Anything**: Tardigrades, tiny microscopic creatures, are nearly indestructible! They can survive extreme heat, cold, intense radiation, and even the vacuum of space. These little critters are often called "water bears."

7. **Octopuses Can Squeeze Through Tiny Gaps**: Octopuses have no bones, which means they can squeeze through the tiniest gaps—sometimes as small as a coin! This ability helps them escape predators and fit into small spaces while hunting for food.

8. **Salmon Use Super Smell to Find Their Way Home**: Salmon are born in rivers and then swim out to sea for most of their lives. When it's time to return and lay eggs, they use their incredible sense of smell to find the exact river where they were born.

9. **Sea Cucumbers Can Turn Liquid**: Sea cucumbers have an amazing defense mechanism—they can liquefy their bodies! By turning their insides into a gooey liquid, they can escape predators by slipping into tight spaces. Once they're safe, they solidify back to their normal form!

10. **Chameleons Change Colors**: Chameleons are famous for their color-changing abilities, but did you know they do this not just for camouflage? They also change colors based on their mood, and temperature, and even communicate with other chameleons!

Fun Fact Quiz

How does the electric eel defend itself?

A. By biting

B. By shocking with up to 600 volts

C. By turning invisible

D. By shooting ink

Strange and Unusual Habitats

1. **Tardigrades Live Almost Everywhere**: Tardigrades, also known as "water bears," can survive in some of the most extreme places on Earth—from the deep sea to the icy Arctic and even in space! These tiny creatures are almost indestructible and can live in habitats no other animal can survive in.

2. **Deep-sea Vents Are Hot Underwater Worlds**: At the bottom of the ocean, there are deep-sea vents that spew out boiling water full of chemicals. Despite the extreme heat and pressure, creatures like giant tube worms and crabs thrive in these strange underwater worlds.

3. **The Canopy of the Amazon Rainforest**: The canopy, or the top layer of the Amazon Rainforest, is home to 90% of its animals! Creatures like monkeys, sloths, and colorful birds rarely

touch the ground and spend their entire lives swinging and flying through the treetops.

4. **Antarctic Lakes Are Full of Life**: Even in freezing Antarctica, there are lakes hidden beneath the ice where strange creatures live. In these icy, pitch-black waters, scientists have found microscopic life that survives without sunlight—living off the chemicals in the water.

5. **The Dead Sea Is Alive**: Despite its name, the Dead Sea isn't completely lifeless. While fish can't survive due to the extreme saltiness, tiny microorganisms like bacteria and algae thrive in these salty waters, making it one of the most unusual habitats on Earth.

6. **Cave Creatures Live in Total Darkness**: In pitch-black caves deep underground, animals have adapted to live without any light. Creatures like blind fish, bats, and strange insects use other senses, like touch and smell, to navigate their dark, isolated homes.

7. **Mangrove Forests Live in Both Salt and Freshwater**: Mangrove trees grow in coastal areas where freshwater meets saltwater, creating a unique habitat. These forests are home to creatures like crabs, fish, and even tigers in some regions, making them one of the most unusual ecosystems in the world.

8. **The Sahara Desert Has Snow**: The Sahara Desert is one of the hottest and driest places on Earth, but did you know it

sometimes gets snow? Although it's rare, snow has fallen in the Sahara, creating a strange sight of white dunes in one of the world's most famous deserts.

9. **Life Exists in Acidic Lakes**: In places like Yellowstone National Park, acidic lakes are home to extremophiles—tiny organisms that can survive in super acidic conditions. These hot, bubbling pools would be deadly for most creatures, but not for these tough little microbes!

10. **Death Zone**: The "Death Zone" on Mount Everest is a deadly habitat where there's so little oxygen that even humans struggle to survive. Yet, some tiny creatures like jumping spiders have adapted to live in this extreme environment at more than 26,000 feet above sea level!

Fun Fact Quiz

Where do most of the animals in the Amazon Rainforest live?

A. On the forest floor

B. In the rivers

C. In the canopy (treetop layer)

D. In caves

Fascinating Marine Animals:

1. **Giant Squids Have Eyes the Size of Soccer Balls**: Giant squids, one of the largest invertebrates in the ocean, have enormous eyes—up to 10 inches across, about the size of a soccer ball! These massive eyes help them see in the deep, dark ocean where very little light reaches.

2. **The Immortal Jellyfish**: Some jellyfish species, like the *Turritopsis dohrnii*, can reverse their aging process and return to their juvenile form! This ability to potentially live forever (unless they are eaten) has earned them the nickname "immortal jellyfish."

3. **Dolphins Can Turn Off Half Of Their Brain**: Dolphins are amazing because they can sleep with only half of their brain at a time! The other half stays awake to help them keep swimming and remain aware of their surroundings. This allows dolphins to rest without ever fully falling asleep.

4. **Pufferfish Inflate Like Balloons**: Pufferfish have an amazing defense mechanism: they can inflate into a spiky ball when they feel threatened. This makes them look much bigger and harder for predators to swallow!

5. **Clownfish Are Protected by Poisonous Anemones**: Clownfish live among sea anemones, which have poisonous tentacles. However, clownfish are immune to the sting of

anemones, and they use the tentacles as a safe home where predators won't dare follow them.

6. **Sea Sponges Are One of the Oldest Living Animals**: Sea sponges may look like simple, plant-like creatures, but they are actually one of the ancient living animals, almost 600 million years old. These fascinating creatures filter water for food and can regenerate lost parts.

7. **Parrotfish Sleep in a Bubble of Mucus**: As the sun sets, parrotfish secrete mucus to form a bubble around themselves and sleep. This 'slime blanket' serves the purpose of odor concealing so that it acts as a shield against hunters and bugs. It may seem odd, but it is a brilliant idea to protect oneself while in the sea!

8. **The Blobfish Lives in Deep Ocean Waters**: The blobfish has a distinct appearance. It lives at extreme depths where the pressure is so high that its body looks more like a blob of jelly! It only appears "blobby" when brought to the surface due to the change in pressure.

9. **Some Sharks Glow in the Dark**: Certain species of sharks, like the swell shark, have bioluminescent skin that glows in the dark. This glowing ability helps them hide from predators by blending in with the glowing ocean below, making them nearly invisible.

Fun Fact Quiz

Which sharks can glow in the dark?

A. The Great White Shark

B. Kitefin Shark

C. Bull Shark

D. Basking Shark

Incredible Animal Adaptations

1. **Penguins Have Built-In "Wetsuits"**: Penguins stay warm in icy waters thanks to their thick layer of blubber and tightly packed, waterproof feathers. These special feathers act like a built-in "wetsuit," trapping air close to their bodies and keeping them warm even in freezing Antarctic temperatures.

2. **Giraffes Have Super-Tough Tongues**: Giraffes have long, tough tongues—about 20 inches long—that help them grab leaves from thorny trees. Their tongues are so strong and thick that the thorns don't hurt them at all!

3. **Archerfish Can Shoot Water**: Archerfish have an incredible hunting skill—they can shoot jets of water at insects above the water's surface. Their accurate water "spit" can knock prey off branches from a distance of over a meter!

4. **Camels Store Fat in Their Humps**: It has always been believed that camels store water in their sack but in actuality they store fats. This fat helps camels survive long periods without food, and when it's used up, their humps can shrink and droop.

5. **Snakes Smell with Their Tongues**: Snakes have a unique way of sensing their environment—they use their tongues to "smell" the air! By flicking their tongues, they pick up scent particles and analyze them using a special organ in their mouths.

6. **Flying Fish Can Glide Over Water**: Flying fish can leap out of the water and glide through the air for distances up to 200 meters! They use their long, wing-like fins to escape predators by gliding over the surface of the ocean.

7. **The Lyrebird Can Mimic Any Sound**: The Australian lyrebird is gifted with an extraordinary talent that allows it to reproduce virtually any sound it perceives. This ability makes it possible for the bird to recreate the sounds of other birds, a camera, a chainsaw, or even a human voice, and this forms part of its prowess as a husbandry expert in the avian world!

Fun Fact Quiz

Where do camels store fat?

A. In their humps

B. In their legs

C. In their stomach

D. In their hooves

Game
Animal Sound Quiz

Roar, meow, and squawk! Let's have some fun with wild and wacky animals. Can you guess which animal makes each sound?

How to Play:

Step 1: Think about some of the animals we talked about—can you make the sounds they make? Let's try it! Can you roar like a lion? Or trumpet like an elephant?

Step 2: If you're with a friend or family member, take turns making animal sounds and guessing what animal the other person is pretending to be!

Step 3: After you guess, share a fun fact about that animal! For example, did you know a lion's roar can be heard from miles away?

Tip: No need for any materials—just use your voice and imagination! Wild animals sure are fun to mimic!

Chapter 3:
Dinosaur Discoveries

Get ready to travel back in time to when dinosaurs ruled the Earth! In this chapter, you'll discover incredible facts about these prehistoric giants. From fierce predators to plant-eating giants, dinosaurs came in all shapes and sizes. We'll explore newly discovered species, learn about life during the age of dinosaurs, and find out how these amazing creatures evolved. Whether you're curious about the biggest meat-eaters or how some dinosaurs may have looked more like birds, this chapter will bring the fascinating world of dinosaurs to life. Prepare for a roaring adventure through the age of dinosaurs!

The Fiercest Predators

1.   **Tyrannosaurus Rex Had a Powerful Bite**: Among all living creatures, the bite force of a T Rex is speculated to be among the highest! The approximate force with which the T. Rex could bite is about 12800 pounds, more than sufficient to crush bones. Such an intimidating predator utilized its jaws to prey upon the large prey with great ease.

2.   **Velociraptors Were Fast and Smart**: Although velociraptors were relatively petite, they were very quick and intelligent! These hunters which could attain speeds of up to 40 mph, hunted in groups and deployed their beaks to grasp prey.

3.   **Allosaurus Had Serrated Teeth**: Allosaurus, the late Jurassic era dinosaur was a terrifying predator known for its sharp and serrated teeth as sharp as a knife used to cut meat. Such types of teeth assisted the dinosaur in slicing meat that was rather tougher and hence, was an efficient killer.

4.   **Carnotaurus Had Horns**: A swift and ferocious carnivore, Carnotaurus possessed two prominent horns over its eyes. Its arms were relatively small, but those horns were probably adapted to defend against other dinosaurs or to attract potential females.

5.   **Giganotosaurus Was a Giant Predator**: Giganotosaurus was a carnivorous dinosaur that was larger even than T. rex! This enormous creature inhabited southern continents and would efficiently hunt in packs against dominantly-sized beings like

Argentinosaurus, which was one of the biggest dinosaurs in South America.

6. **Deinonychus Had Deadly Claws**: A near relative of Velociraptor, Deianuchus had long claws, which were strongly curved, on its feet. It could jump onto its prey and use these claws to inflict fatal cuts – thus, it was one of the most dangerous predators of its period.

7. **Majungasaurus Was a Cannibal**: The tyrant Majungasaurus of Madagascar is also one of the very few dinosaurs who is said to have been a cannibal! It has been explained with the help of fossils that it in all probability fed upon other individuals of its kind.

8. **Mapusaurus Hunted in Packs**: Mapusaurus, an enormous meat-eater from Argentina, is said to have hunted in groups. In unison, these dinosaurs were capable of bringing down even the largest of plant-eaters thereby becoming one of the most fearsome predatory risks in their ecosystem.

9. **Utahraptor Was the Largest Raptor**: The Utahraptor is considered to be the largest member of the Raptor family, measuring almost twenty feet in length. Although said to be a sturdy and powerful carnivore, this predator with enormous and hooked claws used to be really fast and most probably hunted in groups.

Fun Fact Quiz

Which was the largest carnivorous dinosaur, bigger than T. rex?

A. Giganotosaurus

B. Spinosaurus

C. Carnotaurus

D. Utahraptor

New Dinosaur Discoveries

1. **The Tiny Tiniest Dinosaur, Oculudentavis**: Recently, paleontologists discovered *Oculudentavis*, one of the tiniest dinosaurs ever! This dinosaur was about the size of a hummingbird and had sharp teeth, suggesting it was a predator despite its small size.

2. **Feathered Dinosaurs Found in China**: Many new fossils of feathered dinosaurs have been found in China, such as *Sinosauropteryx*. These discoveries show that many dinosaurs, especially smaller ones, likely had feathers, hinting at a closer link to birds.

3. **Dreadnoughtus: A Giant Among Giants**: *Dreadnoughtus*, a newly discovered titanosaur, was one of the largest dinosaurs ever found. Weighing around 65 tons, it was so big that its name

means "fears nothing"! Its discovery helps us understand how massive some dinosaurs were.

4. **The "Hell Heron," Ceratosuchops**: Discovered in the UK, *Ceratosuchops* earned the nickname "Hell Heron" because it likely hunted both on land and in water, much like modern herons. With its long, sharp snout, it could have snatched up fish and small prey from rivers.

5. **The Beaked Dinosaur, Aquilarhinus**: *Aquilarhinus*, discovered in Texas, had a unique "eagle-like" beak, different from other duck-billed dinosaurs. This odd beak shape helped it scoop up plants, giving it an advantage over other herbivores.

6. **Beibeilong: The Giant Dinosaur Egg**: In 2017, researchers discovered the fossilized embryo of *Beibeilong*, a giant dinosaur that laid some of the largest eggs ever found. These eggs could be as big as basketballs, helping us learn more about how dinosaurs reproduced.

7. **Yutyrannus: The Feathered T. Rex Relative**: *Yutyrannus* is a recently discovered relative of the Tyrannosaurus Rex, but with one big difference: it had feathers! This 30-foot-long predator helps scientists understand how feathers might have played a role in the lives of larger dinosaurs.

8. **Cryodrakon: The Frozen Dragon**: *Cryodrakon*, discovered in Canada, was a giant flying reptile with a wingspan as wide as a bus! Though it wasn't technically a dinosaur, its discovery gives

us new insights into the terrifying creatures that ruled the skies during the age of dinosaurs.

9. **Chilesaurus: The Dinosaur That Looks Like a Mix of Many**: *Chilesaurus*, discovered in South America, has features from several dinosaur groups, earning it the nickname "the platypus of dinosaurs." With a mix of carnivorous and herbivorous traits, it puzzled scientists at first.

10. **Carnivorous Dinosaur That Lived in the Arctic**: A discovery revealed that some dinosaurs, like *Nanuqsaurus*, lived in the Arctic. Despite the cold conditions, this small, carnivorous relative of T. rex thrived in the northern regions, giving us clues about how dinosaurs adapted to different climates.

Fun Fact Quiz

Where were many feathered dinosaur fossils recently discovered?

A. India

B. Russia

C. China

D. Pakistan

Life in the Age of Dinosaurs

1. **Earth's Continents Were Once Connected**: During the early age of dinosaurs, all of Earth's land was connected to one giant supercontinent called Pangaea. Over millions of years, it slowly broke apart into the continents we know today.

2. **Dinosaurs Lived Alongside Early Mammals**: Dinosaurs weren't the only creatures around—early mammals also existed, though they were much smaller. Most early mammals were tiny, shrew-like creatures that lived in burrows to avoid becoming dinosaur snacks.

3. **The Weather Was Much Warmer**: The climate during the age of dinosaurs was warmer than it is today. There were no polar ice caps, and the world was covered with lush forests, making it the perfect environment for giant reptiles to thrive.

4. **Giant Insects Ruled the Skies**: Insects were much larger in the age of dinosaurs. Dragonflies had wingspans of over 2 feet, and giant millipedes the size of cars roamed the forests! These massive bugs shared the world with dinosaurs before their sizes shrank over time.

5. **Some Dinosaurs Lived in Herds**: Many plant-eating dinosaurs, like *Triceratops* and *Hadrosaurus*, lived in herds for protection. By sticking together, these herbivores could better defend themselves against large predators like *T. rex*.

6. **Crocodiles Are Descendants Of Dinosaurs**: Crocodiles are the reptiles that survived 65 million years ago. Crocodiles and alligators are descendants of ancient reptiles that lived during the age of dinosaurs, and they've barely changed over millions of years!

7. **Pterosaurs Ruled the Skies**: While they weren't technically dinosaurs, pterosaurs were flying reptiles that soared through the skies during the Mesozoic Era. Some, like *Quetzalcoatlus*, had wingspans of up to 33 feet, making them some of the largest flying creatures ever.

8. **Plant Life Was Different**: The plants during the age of dinosaurs were quite different from today's. There were no flowering plants or grass! Instead, the landscape was covered with ferns, conifers, and giant horsetails.

9. **The Chicxulub Asteroid Ended the Dinosaurs' Reign**: Approximately 65 million years ago, dinosaurs suddenly ceased to exist with the impact of a massive asteroid located in the vicinity of present-day Mexico. This impact caused massive climate changes that led to the extinction of most dinosaurs.

Fun Fact Quiz

Which creatures in modern times are considered descendants of ancient reptiles from the age of dinosaurs?

A. Lizards and snakes

B. Frogs and salamanders

C. Crocodiles and alligators

D. Turtles and tortoises

The Evolution of Dinosaurs

1. **Dinosaurs Evolved from Reptiles**: Dinosaurs evolved from a group of reptiles called archosaurs. These reptiles lived during the Triassic period, and over millions of years, they evolved into the many species of dinosaurs we know today.

2. **Some Dinosaurs Evolved into Birds**: Not all dinosaurs went extinct! Some small, feathered dinosaurs evolved into birds. Modern birds are considered the last living relatives of dinosaurs, showing that not all dinosaurs disappeared.

3. **Feathers Came Before Flight**: Many dinosaurs had feathers, but they didn't all use them for flying. Some dinosaurs used feathers for warmth, display, or camouflage long before any species started flying.

4. **The Earliest Dinosaurs Were Small and Fast**: The first dinosaurs were small, lightweight, and very fast runners. These early dinosaurs, like *Eoraptor*, were much smaller than the giant dinosaurs that appeared later during the Jurassic and Cretaceous periods.

5. **Sauropods Became Giants Over Time**: Sauropods, the long-necked dinosaurs like *Brachiosaurus*, weren't always giants. Over millions of years, they evolved to grow larger and larger, becoming the biggest land animals to ever walk the Earth.

6. **Theropods Gave Rise to T. rex and Birds**: Theropods, a group of two-legged, meat-eating dinosaurs, include both the mighty *Tyrannosaurus rex* and small, bird-like dinosaurs that eventually evolved into modern birds.

7. **Dinosaurs Had Hollow Bones**: Some dinosaurs, like theropods, had hollow bones. This adaptation made their skeletons lighter, helping them run faster or, in the case of bird-like dinosaurs, made it easier for them to fly.

8. **Stegosaurus and Ankylosaurus Shared a Common Ancestor**: Armored dinosaurs like *Stegosaurus* and *Ankylosaurus* evolved from the same group of early dinosaurs. Over time, they developed different forms of protection—*Stegosaurus* with plates and spikes, and *Ankylosaurus* with a clubbed tail and heavy armor.

Fun Fact Quiz

What were the earliest dinosaurs like?

A. Giant and slow

B. Small and fast runners

C. Able to fly

D. Amphibious creatures

Game
Fossil Hunt

Dino-detective alert! It's time to go on a fossil hunt and see which dinosaur bones you can uncover. Ready to dig?

How to Play:

Step 1: On a piece of paper, draw a "dig site" (a square with 4 or 5 sections).

Step 2: Number each section and "hide" a dinosaur fossil by picking a number in your head. Now, it's time to dig!

Step 3: Ask someone to pick a number, and when they choose the right number, reveal the fossil! You could say, "You just found a T-Rex fossil!" or "Look, it's a Triceratops bone!"

Tip: You can take turns hiding and finding the fossils. Don't forget to share some dino facts after each dig!

Chapter 4:
Famous Faces and Scientists

In this chapter, we're diving into the incredible world of famous people and groundbreaking scientists! From the creators of inventions that changed the way we live, to amazing trivia of famous people, and finally to young leaders who were able to change the world around them – welcome to this chapter. This chapter honors those who have contributed to the games, films, and televisions that we watch, as well as those who have explored the earth and made new revelations. Brace yourself to delve deep into the captivating biographies and accomplishments of some of the most well-known figures who ever lived!

Legendary Inventors and Their Creations

1. **The First Computer Program**: Ada Lovelace is viewed as the very first programmer in history, thanks to her mathematical inclination. In the 1800s, she developed codes and techniques for the first supersonic computing machine designed by Charles Babbage, which are still relevant to today's computer programming.

2. **George Washington Carver Revolutionized Agriculture**: George Washington Carver created more than 300 products using peanuts, sweet potatoes, and several other crops, thus assisting farmers in the southern part of the United States in cultivating new kinds of crops and improving the quality of their soil.

3. **Leonardo da Vinci Designed Flying Machines**: Everyone recognizes Leonardo da Vinci as a painter of the Mona Lisa. In addition, Leonardo was a gifted inventor. He drew visions of aircraft and helicopter designs centuries before the machines were created!

4. **Nikola Tesla Invented the AC Electricity System**: Thanks to Nikola Tesla's astounding mind, we know of alternating current (AC) electricity that has enabled electrical wiring in houses and cities across the globe. He also envisioned communication without cables, which would later usher in technology such as Wi-Fi or Bluetooth.

5. **Inventor of the World Wide Web:** As everyone goes on the internet and information becomes easy to access, The World Wide Web was invented by Tim Berners Lee in 1989. His innovation of the internet allows one to visit websites, communicate via e-mails, and interact with people across the world.

6. **Hedy Lamarr Was Both an Actress and an Inventor:** Hedy Lamarr, a well-known actress of the 1940s, was also a co-inventor of a technology that would go on to enhance modern-day Wi-Fi as well as Bluetooth connections! She is credited with the earlier developments of what we now know as wireless communication systems.

7. **Steve Jobs Transformed Technology:** As one of the founders of Apple Inc., Steve Jobs created a plethora of inventions, including the revolutionary iPhone, iPad, and Mac computers. The way Job's visionary ideas made personal technology very user-friendly revolutionized the way people live, work, and interact.

Fun Fact Quiz

What important invention did Garrett Morgan create to make streets safer?

A. The stop sign

B. The traffic light

C. The car brake system

D. The pedestrian crosswalk

Famous Celebrities and Fun Facts

1. **Taylor Swift Wrote Her First Song at Age 12**: Taylor Swift started her music career early! She wrote her first song, called "Lucky You," when she was just 12 years old. Today, she's one of the biggest music artists in the world.

2. **Beyoncé Was in a Girl Group Before Going Solo**: Before becoming a global superstar, Beyoncé was part of the girl group Destiny's Child. They released several hit songs before she launched her incredibly successful solo career.

3. **Emma Watson Graduated from College While Filming**: Emma Watson, who is famously known for playing the role as Hermione in the Harry Potter series, was able to pursue a degree in English Literature and graduated from Brown University, all the while still immersed in playing lead roles in various films.

4. **Justin Bieber Was Discovered on YouTube**: Justin Bieber's big break came when he was discovered by a talent manager through his YouTube videos. From posting covers of popular songs, Bieber became an international pop sensation.

5. **Keanu Reeves Loves Giving Back**: Keanu Reeves is known for being generous. He's secretly donated millions to children's hospitals and cancer research and even gave part of his movie earnings to the crew members on film sets.

6. **Ariana Grande Is Named After a Cartoon Character**: Ariana Grande's parents named her after Princess Oriana from the cartoon *Felix the Cat*. Today, she's known worldwide as a pop superstar with a powerful voice!

7. **Daniel Radcliffe Used to Play Pranks on Set**: Daniel Radcliffe, who played Harry Potter, was a prankster on set. He loved pulling tricks on his co-stars, including hiding phones and changing the language settings to confuse them!

8. **Selena Gomez Is a UNICEF Ambassador**: Besides her acting and music career, Selena Gomez became the youngest-ever UNICEF ambassador at 17. She works to help children around the world get better education, healthcare, and protection.

Fun Fact Quiz

Which girl group was Beyoncé a part of before going solo?

A. The Spice Girls

B. Destiny's Child

C. Little Mix

D. Fifth Harmony

Young Heroes Who Changed the World

1. **Greta Thunberg Inspired Millions to Fight Climate Change**: At the age of only 15, Greta Thunberg initiated a worldwide campaign to create awareness concerning climate change. The 'Fridays for Future' school strike that she led motivated millions of young people around the globe to urge leaders to take action.

2. **Louis Braille Invented the Braille System at 15**: Louis Braille lost his sight at a young age, but that didn't stop him from changing the world. At 15, he invented the Braille reading and writing system for the visually impaired, which is still used today.

3. **Iqbal Masih Fought Against Child Labor**: Iqbal Masih was a child laborer in Pakistan who escaped and became an advocate for children's rights. Though his life was tragically cut short, his

activism brought global attention to child labor, inspiring many to fight against it.

4. **Boyan Slat Invented a Device to Clean the Ocean at Age 16**: Boyan Slat, a young inventor from the Netherlands, designed a device to help remove plastic from the ocean. His creation, which he refers to as "The Ocean Cleanup," is currently addressing one of the major environmental issues of our era.

5. **Ruby Bridges Helped End School Segregation at Age 6**: At the tender age of six in 1960, a brave Ruby Bridges stepped into the hostile environment of a white-only school, thus fighting back the school segregation in America. Her bravery made her an important participant in the Civil Rights Movement.

6. **Nkosi Johnson Fought for the Rights of Children with HIV/AIDS**: Born HIV positive in South Africa, Nkosi Johnson grew up to become one of the most notable advocates for the rights of children infected with HIV / AIDS. There is a battle against the bias relating to the disease that echoes her efforts and aids her even in the position of an illness and advocacy. Nevertheless, she died at age 12.

7. **Ryan Hreljac Built Wells for Clean Water at Age 6**: When he was six years old, Ryan Hreljac initiated a fundraising campaign to dig a well in Uganda for clean water. His zeal and commitment inspired the establishment of Ryan's Well Foundation which still provides clean water to communities across the globe.

Fun Fact Quiz

What is Anne Frank known for writing?

A. A novel about space

B. A famous diary during World War II

C. A book about child labor

D. A science textbook

Pioneering Scientists

1. **Albert Einstein Revolutionized Physics**: The manner in which we perceive space and time was revolutionized by Einstein's theory of relativity. This equation E=mc² established a relationship between matter and energy and became the basis of a number of advancements in science.

2. **Apple Fall And Gravity**: Isaac Newton is well known for his gravity discovery - the force that wedges us on the surface! In what seems to be a folklore, he is said to have developed the concept after observing an apple falling off a tree which prompted him to Research why objects fell to the ground.

3. **Rosalind Franklin Helped Discover DNA's Structure**: Rosalind Franklin was a remarkable scientist who utilized X-ray photographs to disclose the double-helical shape of DNA. This

revolutionized the comprehension of how genes work and how living things are created and sustained.

4. **The Theory of Evolution**: The theory of evolution is primarily credited to Charles Darwin. He was inspired by the various species, especially on the Galapagos Islands, and interpreted patterns of animal adaptations and evolution.

5. **Stephen Hawking Made Groundbreaking Discoveries About Black Holes**: Stephen Hawking was an acclaimed physicist who pioneered the study of black holes and cosmology. Despite suffering from ALS, he achieved immense popularity as one of the most disappearing elders within scientific circles.

6. **Jane Goodall Changed How We Understand Chimpanzees**: Jane Goodall is a revolutionary scientist who has worked extensively in the field of chimpanzees. Her studies discovered that chimpanzees are tool makers and users, have emotional capacity, and live in social structures.

Fun Fact Quiz

What did Stephen Hawking study and make important discoveries about?

A. DNA and genetics
B. Black holes and the universe
C. Gravity and motion
D. Animal behavior

Game
Scientist Scramble

You've learned all about brilliant scientists. Let's see if you can figure out who's who by unscrambling their names!

How to Play:

Step 1: Write down the names of the scientists you learned about in the chapter, but mix up the letters! For example, "LAEBTRE" (for Albert Einstein).

Step 2: Now, try to unscramble each name and figure out who they are!

Step 3: After you guess the name, write down one cool thing that scientists discovered!

Tip: If you're stuck, look back in the chapter for clues. Scientists are some of the coolest puzzle solvers around, and now you are too!

Chapter 5:
Amazing Human Body

Get ready to discover the incredible secrets of the human body! In this chapter, you'll learn about the amazing things our bodies can do, from setting world records to performing everyday miracles. We'll explore fascinating facts about how your senses work, dive into the weird and wonderful functions of your body, and uncover the hidden powers of your brain. Whether it's how fast your heart beats or how your muscles help you move, this chapter will show you just how awesome your body is!

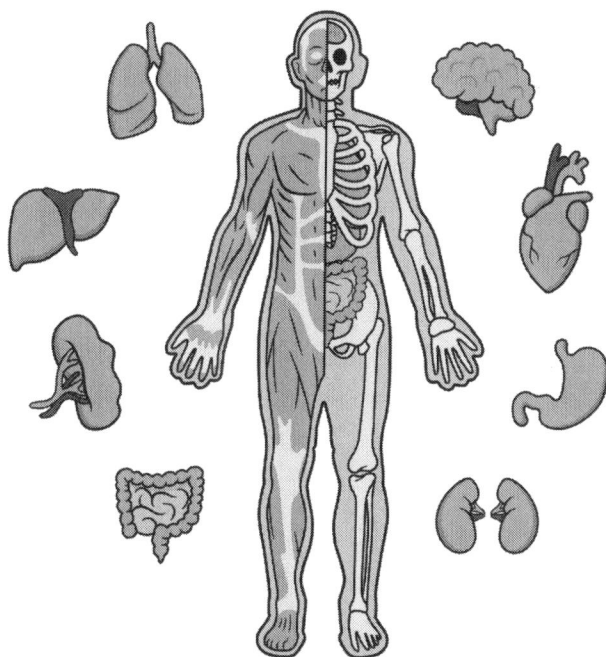

Incredible Body Records

1. **The Longest Time Without Sleep**: The longest recorded time someone went without sleep is 11 days! In 1964, a teenager named Randy Gardner stayed awake for 264 hours as part of a science experiment, showing just how important sleep is for our bodies.

2. **The Fastest Runner in the World**: The record for the fastest sprint for one hundred meters is held by Usain Bolt, who completed the distance in only 9.58 seconds! It was his extreme speed that turned him into a worldwide athletics star and earned him the moniker of "Lightning Bolt."

3. **The Tallest Person Ever**: The tallest person ever recorded was Robert Wadlow, who grew to be 8 feet 11 inches tall! He continued growing throughout his life due to a condition affecting his pituitary gland.

4. **The Most Flexible Person**: Contortionist Daniel Browning Smith holds the record for being the most flexible person. He can twist and bend his body in ways most people can't even imagine, earning him the nickname "The Rubberboy."

5. **The Strongest Bite**: The human with the strongest recorded bite force was Richard Hofmann, whose bite could exert up to 975 pounds of pressure! That's more powerful than some animal bites, like a lion's.

6. **The Longest Finger nails**: The person to hold the record for the longest fingernails ever is Lee Redmond. She grew her nails for over 30 years until they reached a total length of more than 28 feet!

7. **The Loudest Human Scream**: The loudest recorded scream was achieved by Jill Drake, whose voice reached 129 decibels, as loud as a jet engine! Her scream is the loudest ever recorded from a human.

8. **The Most Push-Ups in One Hour**: Australian athlete Jarrad Young set the record for the most push-ups in one hour, completing 3,206 push-ups! His incredible strength and endurance make this record truly impressive.

9. **The Longest Hair**: The longest hair world record is possessed by Xie Qiuping from China. She started growing her hair at the age of 13, and it eventually reached over 18 feet long!

10. **The Fastest Swimmer**: Olympic swimmer César Cielo holds the record for the fastest 100-meter freestyle swim, completing it in just 46.91 seconds. His speed in the water has earned him gold medals and world records.

Fun Fact Quiz

Who was the tallest person ever recorded?

A. Andre the Giant

B. Yao Ming

C. Robert Wadlow

D. Shaquille O'Neal

Secrets of the Human Senses

1. **Your Taste Buds**: Did you know that taste buds are all around in your mouth? You also have taste buds on the roof of your mouth, your throat, and even inside your cheeks!

2. **Your Eyes See Everything Upside Down**: Your eyes see the world upside down! This happens because of the way light enters your eyes and hits the back of your retina. Our brain turns it upside down.

3. **Largest Organ**: The answer to the question of the largest organ is Skin, covering an average of 22 square feet. It protects you from harmful elements, helps regulate body temperature, and even allows you to feel sensations like touch and heat.

4. **You Have Tiny Hairs in Your Ears for Hearing**: Inside your ears, thousands of tiny hair cells help you hear. When sound

enters your ear, these hair cells pick up the vibrations and send signals to your brain, which turns them into sounds.

5. **You Can Only See a Small Part of the Light Spectrum**: Even though it feels like we see everything around us, humans can only see a tiny part of the light spectrum. Animals like bees can see ultraviolet light, while humans can't!

6. **Your Sense of Taste Fades as You Get Older**: As people age, their sense of taste gets weaker. By the time you're 60, you may have lost half of your taste buds, which is why some older adults prefer stronger flavors like spicy foods.

7. **Your Eyes Blink More Than 15,000 Times a Day**: Blinking helps keep your eyes moist and protected from dirt and bright light. Humans blink 15,000 times a day without even realizing it!

8. **Your Ears Help You Stay Balanced**: The tiny semicircular canals inside your ears are responsible for helping you keep your balance. Mobile fluids send signals to your brain about your body's position.

9. **Humans Are Naturally Drawn to Faces**: Your brain is wired to recognize and focus on faces. This is why you can spot a face in a crowd or see faces in objects like clouds or tree bark— your brain loves looking for faces!

Fun Fact Quiz

What is the biggest organ in your body?

A. The Pancreas

B. The heart

C. The skin

D. The brain

Weird and Wonderful Body Functions

1. **You Shed Skin Every Day**: Your skin is constantly renewing itself, and your body gets rid of 30 to 40 thousand dead skin cells per minute! By the end of the year, you've shed almost 9 pounds of skin.

2. **Your Stomach Lining Regenerates Every Few Days**: The acid in your stomach is so strong that it could damage your stomach itself. To protect itself, your stomach lining regenerates every few days, creating a fresh layer of protective cells.

3. **Sneezes Can Travel Up to 100 Miles Per Hour**: When you sneeze, it's like your body's way of clearing out irritants from your nose. Did you know a sneeze can travel at speeds of up to 100 miles per hour? That's faster than a car on the highway!

4. **You Have a Unique Tongue Print**: Just like your fingerprints, your tongue has a unique print! No two people have the same tongue pattern, making it a strange but fascinating part of your identity.

5. **Your Liver Can Regenerate Itself**: The liver is the only organ in your body that can regenerate! If part of it is removed or damaged, the liver can regrow to its full size within a few months, making it a remarkable self-healing organ.

6. **Your Stomach Growls When It's Empty**: The growling sound your stomach makes when you're hungry is called "borborygmi." It happens when your stomach muscles contract to move food and gas through your digestive system—especially when it's empty!

7. **You Can't Breathe and Swallow at the Same Time**: Have you ever tried to breathe and swallow at the same time? It's impossible! That's because your body has a flap called the epiglottis that closes off your windpipe when you swallow, preventing food or liquid from going down the wrong way.

8. **Your Body Contains Gold**: The human body contains trace amounts of gold—about 0.2 milligrams! Most of it is found in your blood, although it's such a small amount that it's not enough to turn you into a millionaire!

9. **Your Brain Makes Electricity**: Your brain generates enough electricity to power a lightbulb! All the signals sent

between neurons in your brain produce electrical energy, helping you think, move, and even dream.

Fun Fact Quiz

What sound is your stomach making when it growls?

A. It's talking to your brain.

B. It's the movement of muscles and gas.

C. It's the acid breaking down food.

D. It's your stomach calling for food.

How the Brain Works

1. **Your Brain Is Like a Supercomputer:** Your brain is incredibly powerful and capable of processing more information than the fastest supercomputers. It contains about 86 billion neurons, which send signals throughout your body to control everything you do.

2. **The Brain Can Generate Dreams:** Every night while you sleep, your brain creates dreams. On average, people dream for about two hours a night, Humans see dreams during REM (Rapid Eye Movement).

3. **Your Brain Works Faster Than You Think:** The brain can send signals through your body at speeds of up to 268 miles per

hour. This allows you to react quickly to things happening around you, like catching a ball or moving away from something hot.

4. **The Brain Changes as You Learn**: Your brain is constantly changing, especially when you learn something new. This process is called neuroplasticity, and it helps your brain grow stronger connections between neurons as you practice new skills or memorize information.

5. **The Brain Never Feels Pain**: Even though the brain processes signals of pain from other parts of your body, it can't feel pain itself. That's because it doesn't have pain receptors like the rest of your body!

6. **Your Brain Can't Multitask Well**: Despite what people might think, your brain isn't great at multitasking. When you try to do two things at once, your brain has to switch back and forth between tasks, which can make you slower and less focused.

7. **Your Brain Shrinks as You Age**: As you get older, your brain slowly shrinks. This is a normal part of aging, but keeping your brain active by learning new things, solving puzzles, or staying curious can help keep it healthy for longer.

8. **The Brain Uses Chemicals to Send Messages**: The brain uses special chemicals known as neurotransmitters to send messages between neurons. These chemicals play a big role in

how you feel, think, and act, helping to regulate mood, sleep, and emotions.

Fun Fact Quiz

During which stage of sleep do most dreams happen?

A. REM (Rapid Eye Movement)

B. Deep sleep

C. Light sleep

D. Daydreaming

Game
Body Part Match

Your body is amazing, and now you get to be the expert! Can you match each body part to what it does? Let's give it a try!

How to Play:

Step 1: On one side of your paper, write down some body parts we talked about (like the brain, heart, and lungs).

Step 2: On the other side, write a short description of what each part does (e.g., "This pumps blood!" or "This helps you breathe!").

Step 3: Now, match each body part with the correct job by drawing a line between them.

Tip: After you match them up, try explaining how each part works to someone else—it's like you're a human body expert now!

Chapter 6:
Epic Moments in History

In this chapter, we'll take a journey through time to explore some of the most important and exciting moments in history! From ancient civilizations that built incredible wonders to inventions that changed the world, you'll discover the stories of heroes, legendary figures, and key events that shaped the course of humanity. We'll also look at the turning points in history where great decisions or actions influenced the future. Get ready to dive into the past and uncover the epic moments that still impact the world today!

Ancient Civilizations and Their Wonders

1. **The Romans Built Roads That Are Still Used Today**: The Roman Empire was known for building thousands of miles of roads to connect its vast territories. Some of these roads are still used today, showing how advanced their engineering was!

2. **The Maya Were Brilliant Astronomers**: The ancient Maya civilization created incredibly accurate calendars by studying the stars. They were so skilled at astronomy that they could predict solar eclipses and other celestial events with precision.

3. **The Colosseum Has The Capacity Of 50,000 People**: The Roman Colosseum, one of the greatest architectural achievements of ancient Rome, could hold over 50,000 people. It served as a venue for gladiatorial contests, wild beast exhibitions, and even staged naval conflicts for the leisure of the masses.

4. **The Terracotta Army Guards an Ancient Emperor**: More than 8,000 life-size terracotta statues of soldiers were buried along with China's first emperor, Qin Shi Huang. This 'Army of Terracotta Figures' was created to be his armed retinue in the afterlife and is known to be one of the most remarkable archaeological findings in history.

5. **The Greeks Were The First To Practice Democracy**: Probably the best and the oldest known example of democracy where citizens participated in the decision-making of their

government is that of ancient Greece. In the city-state of Athens, citizens could vote on important decisions, laying the foundation for modern democracies.

6. **The Indus Valley Civilization Had Advanced Plumbing:** The Indus Valley Civilization, which flourished in modern-day India and Pakistan, had advanced plumbing systems. Their cities had wells, drains, and even early versions of toilets, making them one of the most advanced ancient societies.

7. **The Sphinx of Giza Is Older Than the Pyramids:** The Great Sphinx has the body of a lion and the head of a pharaoh. Construction on it is said to have lasted over a decade around 2500 BCE. Its age is thought to predate the Pyramids of Giza thereby making it one of the oldest colossal statues in the world.

8. **The Historic Sanctuary of Machu Picchu:** The remarkable city of Machu Picchu was constructed by the Incan Empire in the middle of the Peruvian Andes. This 15th-century Inca site is believed to have been a royal or sacred place, leaving the exact reason for its construction a mystery even today.

Fun Fact Quiz

What ancient wonder may have been a myth since no evidence has been found of its existence?

A. The Temple of Artemis

B. The Colossus of Rhodes

C. The Statue of Zeus

D. The Great Pyramid of Giza

Remarkable Inventions That Changed the World

1. **The Wheel Invention**: The wheel is arguably one of the most significant inventions in history. It came to be around 3500 BC, a period that can be said to have witnessed the revolution of movement.

2. **The Telephone Brought the World Closer**: The telephone was invented by Alexander Graham Bell in 1876. This device enabled long-distance conversation among people. Moreover, it became a stepping stone for the modern-day cellular phones and communication networks that exist today.

3. **The Internet Connected the World**: The emergence of the World Wide Web in the late 20th century revolutionized

communicative aspects of human life, also the sources of information. Billions of internet users surf the web for academic research purposes, seek entertainment, and engage in many activities.

4. **Penicillin Was the First Antibiotic**: Thanks to Alexander Fleming's serendipitous discovery in 1928, penicillin became the first antibiotic to be widely used. It transformed medicine for good by eradicating killers that infected many people at some point in history, thus millions of lives were spared.

5. **The Airplane Made the World Smaller**: The Wright brothers invented the first successful airplane in 1903. Their invention changed how people traveled, allowing them to cross oceans and continents in hours rather than weeks or months.

6. **The Light Bulb Brightened Homes**: In 1879, Thomas Edison's invention of the electric light bulb made it possible for everyone to enjoy the benefits of artificial light at night without the need for candles and gas lamps. This invention transformed cities and homes around the world.

7. **The Computer Revolutionized Information**: The invention of computers, starting in the mid-20th century, revolutionized the way people work, learn, and solve problems. From early room-sized machines to today's powerful laptops, computers continue to shape the modern world.

Fun Fact Quiz

What was the first widely used antibiotic that changed medicine?

A. Insulin

B. Penicillin

C. Aspirin

D. Morphine

Heroes and Legends of the Past

1. **Alexander the Great Conquered Much of the Known World**: At just thirty years old, Alexander the Great had already established one of the greatest empires of all time, which extended from Greece to India. His military strategies are still studied today.

2. **Joan of Arc Led Armies at Just 17 Years Old**: Joan of Arc, a young French peasant girl, became a national hero when she led French armies to victory during the Hundred Years' War. She claimed to have been guided by visions and became a symbol of courage and faith.

3. **Robin Hood Was a Legendary Outlaw**: According to legend, Robin Hood was someone who helped the poor as he stole goods from the rich and spread them among the poor. He

lived in Sherwood Forest, stealing from the people of Nottingham. Although we don't know if he was real, his story has been told for centuries.

4.   **Cleopatra is the Most Famous Female Pharoah**: Cleopatra VII was known for her Brains, political skills, and beauty. She formed alliances with the powerful Roman leaders Julius Caesar and Mark Antony, and her life story became a legend after her dramatic death.

5.   **Mulan, A Female Warrior**: In ancient Chinese legend, Mulan was placed in the army as a man to ease her father in old age. She became a legendary warrior and was celebrated for her bravery and loyalty to her family and country.

6.   **King Arthur and the Knights of the Round Table**: The famous legend of King Arthur tells the story of a British king who defended his people from invaders with the help of his knights.

7.   **Hercules Was a Mythical Hero with Incredible Strength**: In Greek mythology, Hercules was known for his incredible strength and courage. He completed 12 labors, which included battling dangerous creatures and completing impossible tasks, making him one of the greatest heroes of all time.

8.   **Gilgamesh Was a Hero from One of the Earliest Legends**: The Epic of Gilgamesh is the story of King Gilgamesh, one of the initial forms of literature, who went on a quest for

immortality. His legendary adventures are filled with gods, monsters, and great battles.

Fun Fact Quiz

Who led a major slave rebellion against the Roman Empire?

A. Spartacus

B. Julius Caesar

C. Alexander the Great

D. King Arthur

Turning Points in History

1. **Roman Empire Changed Europe Forever**: In 476 AD, marked the end of ancient Rome's dominance. It led to the rise of new kingdoms in Europe and shaped the medieval period.

2. **The Discovery of America in 1492 Opened the New World**: Christopher Columbus's voyage in 1492 led to the discovery of the Americas by Europeans. This event changed the course of history by connecting Europe, Africa, and the Americas in trade, culture, and exploration.

3. **The Industrial Revolution Transformed How Goods Were Made**: In the late 1700s, the Industrial Revolution introduced machines that could mass-produce goods. This revolutionized

sectors such as textiles, transport, and production, altering how people worked and lived.

4. **The French Revolution Changed Governments Worldwide**: In 1789, the French Revolution erupted aiming to overthrow the monarchy and replace it with the French Republic. The revolution propagated the unalienable rights of mankind, liberty, equality, and fraternity which changed a lot of other countries.

5. **Magna Carta**: The Magna Carta is a contractual agreement signed in the years after 1215, The document was aimed at diminishing the royal authority and providing freedoms to the people. It is seen as a step towards the development of modern democracy.

6. **The Abolition of Slavery Changed Human Rights Forever**: The cessation of servitude in the 19th century, commencing from the likes of the UK, and the USA, was a breakthrough in human's quest for civil liberties. It eliminated many centuries of unjust treatment and paved the way for contemporary human rights activism.

7. **Changed World's Political Landscape**: The conclusion of World War II in 1945 brought about a new world order in politics. It led to the creation of the United Nations, along with the Cold War, and a new era of international cooperation and rivalry.

Fun Fact Quiz

Who discovered the Americas in 1492, changing the course of history?

A. Vasco da Gama

B. Ferdinand Magellan

C. Christopher Columbus

D. Marco Polo

Game
Time Traveler

Are you ready to travel through time? Let's see if you can match these important moments with the right year!

How to Play:

Step 1: On one side of the page, list some important moments from history (like "First man on the moon").

Step 2: On the other side, write the correct years or periods (like 1969 for the moon landing).

Step 3: Now, match the event with the correct time!

Tip: You're a time-traveling historian now—after you match them, share a quick fun fact about each event. History is full of exciting adventures!

Chapter 7:
Botanical Wonders

In this chapter, we're going to explore the amazing world of plants! The world of plants has in store for us many interesting and unbelievable things including a variety of insect-eating plants to the tallest trees of the world. Get ready to find out about the eccentricities of long-living plants considered to be enchanted, and the remarkable attitudes of vegetation towards their environment. Get ready to dive into the wonders of botany and discover just how extraordinary plants can be!

Carnivorous Plants and Their Prey

1. **The Venus Flytrap Snaps Shut in Less Than a Second**: Among the many plants that consume insects for sustenance, the Venus flytrap stands out. It closes its so-called jaws in under a second upon sensing a bug inside, thus ensnaring the captured bug to swallow it.

2. **Pitcher Plants Turn Insects into Soup**: The vegetative organs of a pitcher plant are used for capturing insects. The bottom of the tube is filled with fluid and the insect that climbs in gets trapped and eventually will be liquefied and absorbed by the plant in a broth of nutrients.

3. **Sundew Plants Use Sticky Tentacles**: Sundew plants feature elongated, moist tendril-like structures on their leaves which glimmer under sunlight to capture bugs. Once an insect makes contact with the adhesive, the tendrils then wrap themselves around the bug pinning it for the purpose of feeding.

4. **The Cobra Lily Uses a Trick**: The Cobra Lily, as its name suggests, looks like a snake and lures insects inside its hooded leaves. However, once the insects enter, they cannot come back out because the walls of the plant are so slimy, and they eventually are digested by the plant.

5. **Bladderworts Trap Prey Underwater**: Bladderworts are a type of carnivorous plant that grows in water. The bladders act

like suction traps that ensnare small water-bearing insects, such as water fleas, in less than a millisecond!

6. **Butterworts Have Leaves That Act Like Flypaper**: Butterworts have sticky, flat leaves that act like flypaper. When an insect lands on them, it gets stuck, and the plant slowly digests it for nutrients.

7. **Tropical Pitcher Plants Can Catch Small Animals**: Some tropical pitcher plants are so large that they can trap not just insects, but also small animals like frogs and even mice! These pitchers hold enough liquid to drown and digest larger prey.

8. **The Waterwheel Plant Is a Rapid Catcher**: The Waterwheel Plant, a cousin of the Venus flytrap, is a fast-acting carnivorous plant. It lives in water and uses snap traps to catch tiny aquatic animals in less than half a second.

9. **The Yellow Pitcher Plant Lures Prey with Nectar**: The Yellow Pitcher Plant produces sweet nectar that attracts insects to its trap. Once the insect crawls inside to get the nectar, it slips and falls into the plant's tube, where it gets trapped and digested.

10. **Some Carnivorous Plants Glow to Attract Prey**: Some carnivorous plants, like the tropical sundew, emit a soft glow under ultraviolet light. This glow attracts insects, making it easier for the plant to catch its next meal.

Fun Fact Quiz

Which plant tricks insects into entering its hooded leaves, trapping them inside?

A. Venus flytrap

B. Cobra Lily

C. Sundew

D. Butterwort

The Oldest and Tallest Trees

1. **Sequoias Can Weigh as Much as a Space Shuttle**: Giant sequoias are not only tall, but they're also incredibly heavy. Some of these trees weigh as much as 2.7 million pounds—about the same weight as a space shuttle!

2. **Baobab Trees Can Store Thousands of Gallons of Water**: Baobab trees, which grow in Africa, can store up to 32,000 gallons of water in their thick trunks. This helps them survive long droughts, making them some of the most resilient trees on Earth.

3. **The Pando Forest Is a Single Giant Organism**: Pando, a forest of quaking aspen trees in Utah, is one enormous organism. All the trees are genetically identical and share the same root

system, making them one of the largest and oldest living organisms on Earth.

4. **The Banyan Tree Has Roots That Grow Above Ground**: Banyan trees are famous for their massive, above-ground roots that spread outwards. These roots can form new trunks, creating the appearance of a tree with hundreds of trunks!

5. **Jaya Sri Maha Bodhi Is a Sacred Tree**: The word renowned Jaya Sri Maha Bodhi tree, which is located in Sri Lanka is one of the most visited trees in the world. It is said to have been planted as a cutting of the tree where Buddha achieved enlightenment more than 2300 years ago.

6. **The Dragon's Blood Tree Resembles an Umbrella**: The Tree of Dragon's Blood which is native to Socotra Island is known for its distinct shape which looks like an umbrella. The red sap that this tree produces has been used for ages both to color and to heal, and the sap is called "dragon's blood".

7. **Olive Trees Can Live for Thousands of Years**: Olive trees are some of the longest-living trees, with some in the Mediterranean being 2,000 years old. These ancient trees still produce olives today!

Fun Fact Quiz

How much water can a baobab tree store in its trunk?

A. 5 thousand gallons

B. 10 thousand gallons

C. 20 thousand gallons

D. 32 thousand gallons

Plants with Magical Properties

1. **Mandrake Roots Were Believed to Scream**: In ancient times, people believed that mandrake roots had magical powers. It was said that when you pulled the plant from the ground, it would let out a terrifying scream that could cause harm to anyone nearby!

2. **Aloe Vera Has Been Used for Healing for Thousands of Years**: Aloe vera is often called the "plant of immortality." For thousands of years, it has been used to heal burns, cuts, and skin irritations. Ancient Egyptians even used it in their beauty routines!

3. **Mistletoe Was Considered a Symbol of Protection**: In ancient times, mistletoe was believed to have magical powers to protect people from evil spirits. Druids, the priests of ancient

Celtic culture, used it in ceremonies and rituals for its supposed healing powers.

4. **Ginseng Is Known as an "Energy Root"**: Ginseng has been used in traditional Chinese medicine for over 2,000 years. It's believed to boost energy, improve memory, and reduce stress, earning it the nickname "energy root."

5. **Garlic Was Thought to Repel Vampires**: Garlic has long been believed to have protective powers. In folklore, it was used to repel vampires and evil spirits. People even hung garlic around their homes to keep bad luck and danger away.

6. **Lavender Was Used to Calm the Mind**: For ages, lavender has been employed to ease the mind and facilitate sleep. Even the Romans and the Greeks cooked it for their baths for the purpose of unwinding and calming down at the end of a tiresome day.

7. **Sage Was Believed to Bring Wisdom and Clarity**: Traditionally, sage has represented wisdom and clear thinking. Many civilizations burned sage for the purpose of cleaning a space of negative energy and believed that it improved mental focus and eliminated mental clutter.

8. **Yew Trees Were Considered Sacred in Ancient Times**: In ancient Europe, yew trees were thought to have magical powers and were often planted near sacred sites like churches and cemeteries. The tree was associated with both death and immortality due to its long lifespan.

9. **Henbane Was Used in Magic Potions**: Henbane is a plant that was often used in ancient magic potions. Its leaves contain chemicals that can cause hallucinations, so it was believed to have mystical powers, but it can also be poisonous in high doses!

10. **Rosemary Was Used for Memory Enhancement**: Rosemary has long been associated with memory. In ancient Greece, students would wear garlands of rosemary around their heads while studying, believing it would help them remember their lessons better.

Fun Fact Quiz

Where were yew trees often planted in ancient Europe because of their magical powers?

A. Near schools

B. Near sacred sites like churches and cemeteries

C. In marketplaces

D. On mountain tops

Unusual Plant Adaptations

1. **The Welwitschia Plant Only Grows Two Leaves**: The Welwitschia plant, found in the Namib Desert, has only two leaves that grow continuously throughout its life. Despite living in one of the harshest environments, this plant can live for over 1,000 years!

2. **Mangrove Trees Can Grow in Saltwater**: Mangrove trees have adapted to grow in salty coastal waters. Their roots filter out salt, allowing them to thrive where most plants would not survive. They even help protect coastlines from erosion!

3. **Lithops Look Like Stones to Avoid Being Eaten**: Lithops, also known as "living stones," are small, succulent plants that blend in with the rocks around them. This camouflage helps them avoid being eaten by animals in their natural habitat.

4. **Water Lilies Swim On Water**: Water lilies have large, flat leaves that levitate on the surface of ponds and lakes. Their roots are anchored in the mud below, but their leaves and flowers stay above water to absorb sunlight for photosynthesis.

5. **The Resurrection Plant Can Survive Without Water for Years**: The Resurrection Plant, found in desert regions, can survive for years without water. When it's dry, it curls up into a brown ball, but when it gets water again, it "comes back to life," turning green and unfurling its leaves.

6. **Venus Flytraps Can Count**: Venus flytraps can actually "count" to ensure their prey is trapped. After a bug touches its sensitive hair twice, the plant snaps shut. This prevents the plant from closing unnecessarily if debris or rain touches it.

7. **The Corpse Flower Smells Like Rotten Meat**: The Corpse Flower produces one of the worst smells in nature, similar to rotten meat. This odor attracts flies and beetles, which help pollinate the plant. Despite the smell, the Corpse Flower only blooms once every few years!

8. **The Sensitive Plant Closes Its Leaves When Touched**: The Sensitive Plant, or Mimosa pudica, reacts to touch by quickly closing its leaves. This defense mechanism helps it avoid being eaten by animals, as the sudden movement can startle predators.

Fun Fact Quiz

Why are Lithops also called "living stones"?

A. They grow inside rocks.

B. They look like stones to avoid being eaten.

C. They grow very slowly.

D. They have a stone-like texture.

Game
Grow Your Garden

Plants need a lot of love and care to grow. Now it's your turn to grow your very own garden!

How to Play:

Step 1: Draw a little plant on your paper (a small seed or sprout).

Step 2: Answer some plant-related questions to "grow" your garden. For example, "What do plants need to grow?" (Answer: Sunlight, water, soil!)

Step 3: For each correct answer, add something to your drawing, like leaves or flowers, until your garden is full!

Tip: Keep your garden growing by learning more about plants. The bigger your garden, the more of a plant expert you become!

Chapter 8:
Mind-Blowing Technology

In this chapter, we'll explore some of the most amazing and futuristic technologies that are changing the world! From robots that can think and act on their own to gadgets that fit in your pocket but have the power of a supercomputer, technology is evolving faster than ever before. You'll learn about the latest inventions, how artificial intelligence is shaping the future, and the exciting world of virtual reality. Get ready to dive into the incredible innovations that are making the impossible possible!

The World of Robots and AI

1. **Robots Are Being Used to Explore the Ocean:** While humans can't easily reach the deepest parts of the ocean, robots can! Underwater robots, like remotely operated vehicles (ROVs), are sent deep into the ocean to explore shipwrecks, study marine life, and map the ocean floor, places too dangerous for humans to explore.

2. **Some Robots Can Learn Like Humans:** AI-powered robots can "learn" by processing data and adjusting their behavior. This ability is called machine learning, and it allows robots to get better at tasks over time, much like humans improve with practice.

3. **Sophia the Robot Can Hold a Conversation:** Sophia is one of the most advanced humanoid robots in the world. Her talking, facial expressions, and even answering through AI in her make her appear sort of human!

4. **Robots Can Perform Surgery:** Now there are even robots that shoulder the responsibilities of the surgeon and these robots are quite accurate. Robotic surgery helps minimize risks and may even Enable the doctor to perform surgery from a remote place with robotic arms.

5. **AI Can Predict the Weather:** The help of artificial intelligence in the analysis of vast amounts of weather data provides meteorologists with the ability to forecast storms,

hurricanes, and even more complicated weather patterns with a higher degree of efficiency than previously experienced.

6. **Robots Are Used in Factories Around the World:** Numerous manufacturing plants incorporate robotics in the production of vehicles, electronic devices, and a plethora of other commodities. These machines operate at a much faster pace than human beings and hence, assist in mass production of goods in less time than what a person would do.

7. **AI Can Help Translate Languages:** Translation services offered by AI programs such as Google Translate, are an important tool that can transform one language into another almost instantaneously allowing people from different quarters of the world to interact with much ease.

8. **Robots Are Helping in Disaster Zones:** In disaster-prone regions such as those affected by earthquakes and hurricanes, robots are deployed to look for survivors, remove debris, and even transport goods. These rescue machines can venture into areas that are too hazardous for people, thus enhancing their worth in missions that are aimed at saving lives.

9. **AI Helps Self-Driven Cars:** Artificial intelligence is incorporated in self-driving vehicles, which aids them in 'seeing' the road, steering clear of barriers, and obeying traffic rules. These vehicles are still undergoing trials, however, one day they might be common means of transport.

10. **AI Can Create Music and Art:** From composing music to painting and writing, artificial intelligence has touched almost all aspects of human creativity. Though robots and AI don't experience emotions as humans do, they are still capable of producing creative artwork through logic and data.

Fun Fact Quiz

How is AI used in weather forecasting?

A. It controls the weather.

B. It analyzes data to predict storms and weather patterns.

C. It creates weather patterns.

D. It reads people's minds to guess the weather.

Cool Gadgets of the Future

1. **Smart Glasses Can Show You Information Right in Front of Your Eyes:** Similar to those that are under development by various tech giants, smart glasses can overlay information, maps, or even text messages directly in the user's line of vision. It's like having a tiny screen on your glasses!

2. **3D Printers Can Create Almost Anything:** Building layers gradually involves the use of third-dimensional printers with specific materials such as plastic or metals. They are making everything from fiberglass toys to entire houses and even manufacturing components for vehicles and aircrafts!

3. **Smartwatches Can Track Your Health:** The latest smartwatches are growing in sophistication and feature heart rate, step and sleep monitoring, and even notifications in the event of an anomaly. It's like having a health monitor very close to the wrist!

4. **Drones Can Deliver Packages to Your Door:** There are possibilities in the future where drones might come and deliver packages to one's doorstep. Currently, drone deliveries are being tested by some companies; hence, ordering items online can even be quicker and more efficient than ever.

5. **Virtual Reality Headsets Can Transport You Anywhere:** Thanks to the advent of virtual reality (VR) headsets, audiences can experience events and explore new places without having to physically step outside the comfort of their homes.

6. **Self-Lacing Shoes Are Real:** The concept of self-lacing shoes was inspired by motion pictures. In the present times, these shoes are a reality. Self-lacing shoes are advanced-designed shoes in which the laces operate automatically according to the comfort of the wearer.

7. **Smart Refrigerators Can Help You Manage Groceries:** Today's cutlery includes refrigerators that connect to your mobile phone and provide an insight into their contents without the need to open the door. They can even offer you recipes using the available ingredients in your home or alert you when certain items are almost gone.

8. **Wearable Fitness Trackers Are Getting Smarter:** Fitness trackers, which you wear on your wrist, are becoming smarter and more advanced. They can track not only your steps but also your heart rate, calories burned, and even your stress levels.

9. **Robot Pets Are Getting More Lifelike**: Robot pets, like robotic dogs and cats, are becoming more lifelike. These smart pets can respond to touch, play games, and even learn tricks, providing companionship without the need for feeding or walks.

10. **Flying Cars May Soon Become a Reality**: While it sounds like something out of a sci-fi movie, companies are developing flying cars that could be used in the near future. These vehicles would combine driving and flying, helping people avoid traffic jams and travel faster!

Fun Fact Quiz

What can smart refrigerators do?

A. Play music

B. Show you what's inside without opening the door

C. Cook food

D. Change colors

Inventions That Transformed Our Lives

1. **The Microwave Made Cooking Faster:** The microwave oven was invented by Percy Spencer in 1945, transformed how people cook. It uses microwave radiation to heat food quickly, making it possible to warm up meals in just a few minutes, which changed how we prepare food at home and in restaurants.

2. **The Smartphone Combined Multiple Devices Into One:** The invention of the smartphone revolutionized the way we communicate, work, and play. Combining a phone, camera, computer, and more, smartphones put the power of multiple devices in our pockets, connecting us to the world in an instant.

3. **Electric Cars Are Transforming Transportation:** Electric cars, powered by rechargeable batteries instead of gasoline, are changing the way we think about transportation. These eco-friendly vehicles produce zero emissions, helping reduce pollution and fight climate change.

4. **The Radio Made Information and Music Accessible Everywhere:** The invention of the radio in the late 19th century allowed people to listen to music, news, and stories from all over the world. Long before the advent of television or the internet, radios were already present in the home and had become an integral source of entertainment.

5. **Vaccines Revolutionized Public Health:** The invention of vaccines has saved countless lives by preventing diseases like

smallpox, polio, and measles. Seeing that the initial vaccine was invented by Edward Jenner in 1796, vaccination has changed the dynamics of public health in averting the deadly bacteria.

6. **The Refrigerator Changed Food Storage:** The invention of the refrigerator in the early 20th century changed how we store food. In the past, before the advent of fridges, most people used ice or salt to keep their food from spoiling. Today Refrigerators help in saving food for longer periods thereby decreasing wastage and simplifying the food storage process.

7. **The Electric Washing Machine Made Laundry Easier:** The invention of the electric washing machine transformed how people do laundry. If one had to wash clothes before, it was much messier and tiring, whereas with the electric washing machine, one can wash clothes in a much easier, faster, and less exhausting manner. In fact, saving people hours of work every week.

8. **GPS Changed How We Navigate:** The Global Positioning System (GPS), invented in the 1970s, transformed how we navigate. Satellites that orbit the globe have proven to help enable people to determine their locations on digital maps and show exact positions making losing one's way a thing of the past.

9. **Television Brought the World to Our Living Rooms:** The early 20th century brought with it the invention of the television which had a significant impact on the way news, entertainment as well as events are experienced by people. It allowed people to see things happening around the world right from their living rooms.

10. **The Internet Connected the World:** The invention of the internet in the 1960s revolutionized how people communicate and share information. It allows people to send messages instantly, access a vast amount of knowledge, and connect with others globally. Today, the internet is a vital part of everyday life, powering everything from social media to online shopping.

Fun Fact Quiz

Which invention combines a phone, camera, computer, and more into one device?

A. Laptop

B. Tablet

C. Smartphone

D. Smartwatch

Virtual Reality and Augmented Experiences

1. **Virtual Reality Can Take You Anywhere:** With virtual reality (VR), you can visit places like the bottom of the ocean, the top of Mount Everest, or even Mars—all from your living room! Virtual reality headsets allow you to inhabit these fictive universes as if you were actually present there.

2. **Augmented Reality Adds to Your World:** In contrast to VR, which immerses you into a distinct location, augmented reality (AR) enhances the existing environment with virtual

elements. For instance, applications such as Pokémon GO allow users to view various characters and items in the physical space using the camera of their mobile devices.

3. **VR Is Used for Training Astronauts:** Before venturing into outer space, astronauts undergo training using the virtual reality technology at NASA. Instances such as repairs and spacewalks can be practiced using space environment simulation thus, training for the real activities.

4. **Augmented Reality Helps Surgeons Perform Complex Operations:** Surgeons are employing augmented reality to visualize a 3D representation of the organ of the patient being operated upon. This helps doctors carry out intricate surgeries more effectively and accurately.

5. **You Can Explore Ancient Civilizations with VR:** You can literally go back in time with Virtual reality! Look at some VR programs such as exploring Ancient Egypt or Rome in which one can walk through the cities and experience the lives of the people who lived thousands of years back.

6. **AR Can Help You Learn:** To make education more engaging and modern, augmented reality has entered the school system. For instance, AR applications allow students to learn about the solar system with 3-D floating planets in their classrooms, enhancing the lessons and making them more enjoyable.

7. **VR Can Help Treat Phobias:** Therapy has started utilizing virtual reality to help individuals with phobias treat them. V-R takes fear evocation a step further where controlled psychologists help patients face their fears using exposure therapy principles in a digital interface.

8. **AR Can Turn Your Car into a Smart Vehicle:** Some cars now use augmented reality to display important information on the windshield, like navigation directions or the speed limit. This helps drivers keep their eyes on the road while still seeing important details.

9. **You Can Play Sports in VR:** VR allows you to play sports like tennis, basketball, and even boxing without leaving your home. The virtual environment makes you feel like you're on a real court or field, and you can even compete with others online.

10. **AR Is Changing How We Shop:** Augmented reality is being used in online shopping to help customers "try on" clothes or see how furniture would look in their homes before buying. This makes it easier to choose the right items without going to a store.

Fun Fact Quiz

What does augmented reality (AR) add to your world?

A. Extra colors

B. Digital elements like characters or objects

C. Sound effects

D. Virtual pets

Game
Invention Scramble

Technology changes the world! Now, let's see if you can unscramble these inventions and learn how they work.

How to Play:

Step 1: Write down the names of some inventions from this chapter, but scramble the letters (like "TCLIEPBLO" for "Television").

Step 2: Unscramble the letters to figure out the invention.

Step 3: After you guess, write down one cool fact about how that invention changed the world!

Tip: Inventions are all around us! Look around the room to see what cool inventions you can spot.

Chapter 9:
Legends and Myths

Welcome to the world of legends and myths, where imagination runs wild, and stories of heroes, gods, and magical creatures come to life! In this chapter, we'll explore fascinating tales from different cultures around the world, filled with mysterious creatures, powerful gods, and brave heroes. You'll learn about the myths that people once believed in to explain natural events, the origins of legendary creatures like dragons and unicorns, and the timeless stories of heroism and adventure that continue to inspire us today. Get ready to step into a world where anything is possible!

Mythical Creatures and Beasts

1. **Dragons Are Found in Myths Around the World:** From Europe to China, dragons are one of the most popular mythical creatures. In European legends, they are often fierce, fire-breathing monsters, while in Chinese mythology, they are wise and benevolent creatures that bring good fortune.

2. **Unicorns Are Symbols of Purity:** The unicorn is a legendary horse-like creature with a single spiral horn. In myths, unicorns are often depicted as gentle and pure, and they can only be tamed by someone with a pure heart.

3. **The Minotaur Was Half-Man, Half-Bull:** The Minotaur, from Greek mythology, had the body of a man and the head of a bull. It lived in a labyrinth and was known for its terrifying strength. The hero Theseus eventually defeated it.

4. **Banshees Are Ghostly Figures from Irish Folklore:** In Irish folklore, Banshees are ghostly women who are believed to warn families of approaching death by wailing or crying. Despite their eerie presence, they are not evil, but rather messengers.

5. **The Sphinx Is a Guardian with Riddles:** The Sphinx, with the body of a lion and the head of a human, is a famous creature from ancient Egyptian and Greek mythology. It was known for challenging travelers with difficult riddles, and those who failed to answer were said to face dire consequences.

6. **The Chupacabra Is a Modern Mythical Creature:** The Chupacabra is a modern-day mythical creature, first reported in the 1990s in Latin America. It is said to be a strange, reptile-like creature that attacks livestock, particularly goats, and its name means "goat-sucker" in Spanish.

Fun Fact Quiz

What did the Sphinx do to travelers in mythology?

A. It granted them wishes.

B. It asked them riddles.

C. It gave them gold.

D. It turned them into animals.

Ancient Legends from Around the World

1. **The Legend of King Arthur and Excalibur:** In British legends, King Arthur was a great king who ruled Camelot and fought off invaders with the help of his magical sword, Excalibur. It's said that only Arthur could pull the sword from the stone, proving he was the rightful king.

2. **The Epic of Gilgamesh is One of the Oldest Legends:** The Epic of Gilgamesh, from ancient Mesopotamia, is one of the oldest written stories in the world. It tells the tale of King

Gilgamesh and his adventures as he seeks immortality and faces gods and monsters along the way.

3. **The Japanese Legend of the Sun Goddess Amaterasu:** In Japanese mythology, Amaterasu is the goddess of the sun. One famous legend tells how she hid in a cave after being angered by her brother, causing the world to fall into darkness. The other gods had to coax her out to bring back the light.

4. **The Mayan Legend of Kukulkan, the Feathered Serpent:** Kukulkan, the feathered serpent god, was an important deity in Mayan mythology. According to legend, Kukulkan taught the Maya people about architecture, farming, and civilization. He was worshipped as a god of wisdom and wind.

5. **The Chinese Legend of the Monkey King:** The Monkey King, Sun Wukong, is a mischievous and powerful character from Chinese mythology. He could transform into anything, fly on clouds, and fight off enemies with his magical staff. His adventures are told in the famous story *Journey to the West*.

6. **The Egyptian Legend of Osiris:** Osiris, the god of the afterlife in Egyptian mythology, was murdered by his brother Set. However, his wife, Isis, brought him back to life. Osiris then became the ruler of the underworld, overseeing the souls of the dead.

7. **The Legend of Maui, the Demigod from Polynesian Mythology:** In Polynesian mythology, Maui is a trickster

demigod who used his magical fishhook to pull islands from the sea and slow down the sun so that people could have longer days. His cleverness and bravery made him a beloved hero in many Polynesian cultures.

Fun Fact Quiz

Which ancient story is one of the oldest written legends in the world?

A. The Epic of Gilgamesh

B. The Iliad

C. Beowulf

D. The Odyssey

Famous Heroes and Their Stories

1. **Sir Lancelot, the Knight of the Round Table:** Sir Lancelot, one of King Arthur's most trusted knights, was known for his bravery, skill in battle, and loyalty. His love for Queen Guinevere caused conflict, but he remained one of the greatest knights in Arthurian legends.

2. **Atalanta, the Swift-Running Heroine:** In Greek mythology, Atalanta was a swift and skilled hunter. She helped slay the Calydonian Boar, a dangerous creature terrorizing the

countryside. Known for her speed, she challenged any suitor to a footrace, only marrying the one who could beat her.

3. **Sigurd, the Dragon Slayer of Norse Mythology:** Sigurd, a hero in Norse mythology, is famous for slaying the dragon Fafnir. After defeating the beast, Sigurd gained great power and wisdom by tasting the dragon's blood, becoming one of the most legendary figures in Norse sagas.

4. **Arjuna, the Hero of the Mahabharata:** In the ancient Indian epic, the *Mahabharata,* Arjuna was one of the protagonists with great archery and warfare skills. With the guidance of Krishna, he was a participant in the grand war of Kurukshetra fighting to restore Dharma in one of the longest epics written in the world.

5. **Samson, the Strongman from the Bible:** Samson was a Biblical hero, famous for his enviable power which was drawn from his long and unshorn hair. Many other valiant deeds were done by him, such as killing a host of men with the jawbone of an ass, before being betrayed and subsequently losing his powers only to reclaim them in a final bout of bravery.

6. **Jason and the Quest for the Golden Fleece:** According to Greek mythology, the chief of the Argonauts named Jason led an expedition in search of a mythical Golden Fleece, which was considered a token of authority and kingship. His trip was filled with deadly obstacles, including a fight with the harpies and

sailing in dangerous waters, all with the assistance of a witch named Medea.

7. **Cú Chulainn, the Hero of Irish Mythology:** In Irish mythology, Cú Chulainn is depicted as an impressive hero who possesses unnatural power and fury for battle. In the Táin Bó Cúailnge, which is one of the greatest epic tales of Ireland, he was said to have protected the kingdom of Ulster from the invading forces all by himself.

8. **Enkidu, Gilgamesh's Loyal Companion:** The character of Enkidu, in the Epic of Gilgamesh, originates as a savage but learns to dedicate himself to Gilgamesh. They, however, do not stay in peace for long as they engage in fierce monster-fighting adventures in pursuit of fame until the death of Enkidu which teaches Gilgamesh how to appreciate friends and the shortness of human life.

Fun Fact Quiz

What did Perseus use to defeat Medusa without looking directly at her?

A. A magical sword

B. A mirror-shield

C. A helmet of invisibility

D. A bow and arrow

Game
Mythical Creature Match

It's time to dive into the world of myths and legends. Can you match these mythical creatures to their stories?

How to Play:

Step 1: Write down the names of some mythical creatures (like Dragon, Unicorn, Minotaur).

Step 2: Next to each name, write the legend or culture they belong to (like Dragon → China).

Step 3: Draw lines to match each creature with its story. Afterward, share one cool fact about the myth!

Tip: Myths are like ancient stories that live forever—now you know some of the most legendary ones!

Chapter 10:
Amazing Feats and Records

In this chapter, kindly join me and journey into what I consider the greatest human records and, of course, the marvels of nature! Be ready for the unbelievable- sports legends, unbelievable animals, and unbelievable views, including such wonders that conquered the tops of world records and the laws of physics. Whether it is the last lap, the highest leap, or even in the face of the tallest cliff, these are stories of the brave and the dauntless. You are now ready to embark on this exciting quest which will allow us to trace the development of boundaries that have been made by people and solved by nature!

Incredible Human Achievements

1. **Usain Bolt Is the Fastest Man in the World:** This sports hero known as Usain Bolt these days holds the record for the world's fastest 100-meter sprint with 9.58 seconds. He nicknamed him 'Lightning Bolt' based on his speed and performance as one of the finest sprinters in history.

2. **Felix Baumgartner's Space Jump:** In the year of 2012, Austrian skydiver Felix Baumgartner made a historic jump by ascending to 128k feet, which is the equivalent of two and a half times the height of Mount Everest and jumping from that height. His flight was continuing at a supersonic speed, and thus, he became the first man in history to become airborne without any vehicle.

3. **The Longest Marathon:** Dean Karnazes was able to run continuously for 80 hours and 44 minutes to complete the distance of 350 miles without any rest. He surpassed records by running for over 26 hours, thus breaking the record for the longest continuous run.

4. **The Deepest Free Dive:** The record for the deepest free dive is held by Herbert Nitsch, who has dived a distance of 702 feet in the sea without an oxygen tank. His dive is known as "The Deepest Man on Earth" and it reached the limits of physical endurance.

5. **The Longest Time Spent in Space:** Russian cosmonaut Valeri Polyakov remains in space for 437 consecutive days and 18 hours as part of the crew of the Mir space station. His mission proves innocent but still offers important information regarding the adjustments the human body undergoes in the process of space travel.

6. **The Fastest Marathon by a Woman:** In 2019, Brigid Kosgei was the fastest woman to complete a marathon when she did it within 2 hours, 14 minutes, and 4 seconds at the Chicago Marathon. Her performance broke the record by a minute and thirty-five seconds.

7. **The Highest Skydive:** The current record holder of the highest skydive is Alan Eustace - a former Google employee – who carried out the jump in 2014. He free-fell through the Earth's atmosphere and established a new record in extreme sport skydiving at 135,889 feet.

Fun Fact Quiz

Which is the tallest building in the world?

A. Eiffel Tower

B. Burj Khalifa

C. Empire State Building

D. Shanghai Tower

Sports and Stunts That Made History

1. **Jesse Owens' Historic Olympic Victory:** In the 1936 Olympics, Jesse Owens made history by winning four gold medals in track and field, defying Nazi ideology in front of Adolf Hitler. His incredible performance on the world stage became an iconic moment in sports history.

2. **Tony Hawk Lands the First 900:** Skateboarding legend Tony Hawk became the first person to land a "900," a trick involving two and a half spins in the air. He achieved this feat at the X Games in 1999, making it a defining moment in extreme sports.

3. **Roger Bannister Breaks the 4-Minute Mile:** In 1954, Roger Bannister became the first person to run a mile in under four minutes, a feat once thought impossible. His record-breaking time of 3:59.4 changed the landscape of middle-distance running forever.

4. **Simone Biles Dominates Gymnastics:** American gymnast Simone Biles has made history by winning 32 Olympic and World Championship medals. Known for her incredible strength, grace, and ability to perform difficult moves, she is widely regarded as the greatest gymnast of all time.

5. **Evel Knievel's Daring Stunts:** Evel Knievel was a famous stuntman known for his daring motorcycle jumps. One of his most famous stunts was jumping over 13 buses at London's

Wembley Stadium in 1975, making him a legend in the world of extreme stunts.

6. **Usain Bolt's Triple-Triple Olympic Victory:** Usain Bolt is the only sprinter in history who has managed to win three successive Olympic championships in the 100m, 200m, and 4 x 100m relay categories in 2008, 2012, and 2016.

7. **Felix Baumgartner's Freefall from Space:** In 2012, Felix Baumgartner set a world record for the highest skydive, jumping from 24 miles above Earth. He reached speeds of over 800 miles per hour during his freefall, breaking the sound barrier.

Fun Fact Quiz

Which athlete holds the record for the most Olympic medals with 28?

A. Usain Bolt

B. Mark Spitz

C. Michael Phelps

D. Ian Thorpe

Unbelievable World Records

1. **The World's Tallest Man:** The tallest man ever recorded was Robert Wadlow, who stood an incredible 8 feet 11 inches tall. His extraordinary height was caused by a rare condition, and he continues to hold the record for the tallest human in history.

2. **The Longest Fingernails Ever:** Lee Redmond holds the record for the longest fingernails ever on a pair of hands. She stopped cutting her nails in 1979, and by the time they were measured in 2008, they had reached a total length of 28 feet 4 inches!

3. **The Largest Pizza Ever Made:** The largest pizza ever made was 13,580 square feet, created in Rome in 2012. Named "Ottavia," the massive pizza was gluten-free and covered with tons of delicious toppings, making it big enough to feed thousands of people.

4. **The World's Oldest Person:** Jeanne Calment of France holds the record for the longest confirmed human lifespan, living to an astonishing age of 122 years and 164 days. She witnessed more than a century of history and continues to hold this unbelievable record.

5. **The Most Expensive Painting Ever Sold:** Leonardo da Vinci's painting *Salvator Mundi* holds the record for the most expensive painting ever sold, fetching a staggering $450.3 million

at auction in 2017. This masterpiece became the most valuable piece of art in history.

6. **The World's Heaviest Pumpkin:** The heaviest pumpkin ever grown weighed an astounding 2,702 pounds. Grown by a Belgian farmer in 2021, this giant pumpkin set a new world record for the heaviest ever recorded.

7. **The Longest Time Holding a Plank:** George Hood, a former Marine, set the world record for the longest time spent holding a plank. In 2020, he held the position for an incredible 8 hours, 15 minutes, and 15 seconds, setting a new benchmark for fitness enthusiasts.

8. **The Most Spoons Balanced on a Body:** Dalibor Jablanovic from Serbia holds the quirky record for balancing the most spoons on his body—79 spoons in total! He used his head, arms, chest, and back to set this strange but fun world record in 2016.

Fun Fact Quiz

Where was the largest pizza ever made?

A. New York

B. Rome

C. Tokyo

D. Chicago

Game
Record-Breaker Quiz

Are you ready to test your knowledge about the most amazing world records? Let's see if you can guess the right one!

How to Play:

Step 1: Write down three fun facts, but only one of them is a real-world record.

Step 2: Ask someone to guess which one is the record. For example, "Which is the tallest building? Is it A, B, or C?"

Step 3: Reveal the answer and share a fun fact about the record!

Tip: It is also fun as you can create your own record-breaking facts to tell other people. Well, maybe one day you will also set a record, right?

Chapter 11:
Fun and Games

Prepare yourselves for an exhilarating journey into the realms of play. Here in this chapter, we shall find out the history of toys and games, record-breaking facts about play, and funny play practices across the world. Thus, ever since the dawn of time, people have always eagerly sought and never ceased to invent ways to entertain themselves through any means possible. You will also learn of new games and sports that are trending today. If you like sports, if you are a fan of puzzles, or if you enjoy video games, this chapter is filled with fun extras.

Origins of Popular Toys and Games

1. **Monopoly Was Originally Created to Teach Economics:** Monopoly was designed by Elizabeth Magie in 1903 as "The Landlord's Game," but was commercialized as Monopoly by Charles Darrow in 1935. It was originally intended to educate the public on economics and why monopolies are a bad thing. Today, Monopoly is a part of family nights and people actually look forward to playing this game.

2. **The Yo-Yo Dates Back to Ancient Greece:** A toy that continues to entice children of all ages even to this day is the humble yo-yo which was invented more than 2,500 years ago. The ancient Greek kids also had some toys: wooden yo-yos, and these toys remain contemporary with new stunts and models.

3. **Rubik's Cube Was Invented as a Teaching Tool:** The Rubik's Cube, which was invented in 1974, was designed by the Hungarian architect ErnőRubik, with the primary purpose of helping learners solve 3D geometry problems. It rose to world fame and invited millions of people to try untwining its colorful conundrum.

4. **Play-Doh Was Originally a Wallpaper Cleaner:** Play-Doh, a modeling clay, was created in the 1930s as a wallpaper cleaner. It was not like this for children, it became a children's toy in the 50's, and children have brought it out to model dinosaurs and pretend pizza among other things.

5. **Chess Is Over 1,500 Years Old**: One of the oldest strategy games in the world known as chess originated in India more than 1500 years ago. Initially called "chaturanga," this game went global and remains one of the most popular board games to date.

6. **Jenga Was Invented by a Woman from Africa**: The classic block-stacking game Jenga was invented by Leslie Scott, who grew up in East Africa. She created the game using wooden blocks, and it has since become a popular game of skill, focus, and balance.

7. **Twister Was Called "Pretzel" at First**: The famous game Twister, where players place their hands and feet on colored dots, was originally called "Pretzel." It was created in 1966 and became an instant hit, especially after it appeared on *The Tonight Show.*

Fun Fact Quiz

What was the original purpose of the Rubik's Cube?

A. To teach math

B. To teach 3D geometry

C. To solve puzzles

D. As a stress-relief toy

World Records in Sports and Play

1. **Longest Basketball Shot Ever Made:** The longest basketball shot ever made was from an incredible distance of 177 feet, 9 inches (54.26 meters), achieved by Thunder Law from the Harlem Globetrotters in 2016.

2. **Most Consecutive Soccer Ball Juggles:** Milene Domingues holds the world record for the most consecutive soccer ball juggles by a female, with a staggering 55,198 touches without the ball touching the ground!

3. **Longest Gaming Marathon on a Video Game:** The longest gaming marathon lasted for 35 hours and 35 minutes, achieved by Carrie Swidecki in 2015 while playing *Just Dance*.

4. **Most Hula Hoops Spun at the Same Time:** The record for the most hula hoops spun simultaneously is held by Marawa Ibrahim, who managed to spin 200 hula hoops at once in 2015.

5. **Longest Game of Monopoly:** The longest Monopoly game ever played lasted for 70 straight days! This marathon session set the world record for the longest game of Monopoly in history.

6. **Most Cartwheels in a Row:** The world record for the most consecutive cartwheels is 1,386, set by Ashrita Furman, an athlete famous for holding numerous world records in various categories.

7. **Most Jenga Blocks Removed in One Minute:** The record for the most Jenga blocks removed and stacked in one minute is 33, set by Kelvin Rosario in 2019. His lightning-fast skills in the game of balance and precision earned him this world record.

Fun Fact Quiz

What is the world record for the fastest Rubik's Cube solved?

A. 3.47 seconds

B. 4.22 seconds

C. 5.30 seconds

D. 6.55 seconds

Quirky and Fun Traditions Around the World

1. **Japan's Mochi-Pounding Tradition:** During New Year's celebrations in Japan, families make *mochi,* a type of sticky rice cake, by pounding steamed rice with large wooden mallets. The tradition is called *mochi-tsuki* and brings good fortune for the upcoming year.

2. **Holi – India's Festival of Colors:** Holi is a vibrant festival celebrated across India where people throw colored powders at each other, marking the arrival of spring. Known as the Festival of Colors, it's a joyful celebration filled with music, dance, and a rainbow of colors.

3. **Oktoberfest – Germany's Giant Beer Festival:** Oktoberfest, held in Munich, Germany, is the world's largest beer festival, attracting millions of visitors each year. People wear traditional Bavarian clothes, enjoy live music, and, of course, drink lots of beer. It's a celebration of Bavarian culture!

4. **Thailand's Water Festival (Songkran):** During Songkran, Thailand's New Year celebration, people take part in massive water fights in the streets. Using water guns, hoses, and buckets, everyone joins in on the fun to cool off and celebrate the arrival of the new year.

5. **The Monkey Buffet Festival in Thailand:** In the town of Lopburi, Thailand, a feast is held each year for the local monkey population. Tables are piled high with fruits, vegetables, and treats for the monkeys to enjoy as part of the Monkey Buffet Festival, a tradition to honor the animals.

6. **Switzerland's Cow Parade:** Every year, when Swiss cows return from the Alpine pastures at the end of summer, they are dressed up with flowers and bells for a grand parade through the villages. This tradition, called *Alpabzug*, is a celebration of the cows and their importance to Swiss farming.

7. **The Battle of the Oranges in Italy:** During the Carnival of Ivrea in Italy, participants divided into teams and threw oranges at each other in a friendly battle. The event dates back centuries and is one of Italy's most unusual yet exciting traditions.

Fun Fact Quiz

Which country is famous for celebrating Oktoberfest?

A. Austria

B. Belgium

C. Germany

D. Switzerland

Innovative Games of Today

1. **Fortnite Changed the Gaming World:** Battle Royale format was spearheaded by Fortnite in 2017 and it quickly grew to be one of the most played games in history. This combines construction, planning, and survival elements, which entertain millions of players while changing the face of computer games.

2. **Pokémon GO Made the World Its Playground:** Pokémon GO, launched in 2016, was a prominent example of an AR game in which players catch virtual creatures in the real world. With a smartphone in their hands, half of the players' work is done, as they have to search for and capture creatures from the Pokémon world.

3. **Among Us Brought Social Deduction to the Forefront:** Among Us was launched in 2018 and gained unprecedented popularity in 2020, where people have to act like crew members

or killers. The frauds must hinder the crew's objectives as the other crew members attempt to accomplish tasks and find out who the frauds are.

4. **Beat Saber Combines Music and Fitness:** Another VR game that was launched in 2018 is Beat Saber where the player is tasked with swinging the controller to slice blocks that appear on the screen in time to the music. The game is very enjoyable but at the same time it's a great exercise; it is a perfect blend of fun and exercise.

5. **Roblox Lets Players Create Their Own Games:** Roblox was created in 2006, and it enables users to design their own games or play games that are designed by other users. Currently boasting more than 164 million monthly active users, Roblox fosters creativity and innovation among young game developers.

6. **Super Mario Maker Allows Players to Design Their Own Levels:** Super Mario Maker, which was launched in 2015, enables players to create their own Mario levels and to play new levels designed by others. A game that makes users both designers and players at the same time and opens up a world of creativity.

7. **Fall Guys Is a Game Show in Video Game Form:** Fall Guys: Ultimate Knockout is a multiplayer video game that was launched in the year 2020, where players get to engage themselves in insane obstacle courses and challenges.

8. **VRChat Lets Players Explore Virtual Worlds Together:** VRChat is an online platform that lets users explore 3D virtual worlds and interact with others in real time. Players can design their own avatars and create custom worlds, offering a unique social experience in virtual reality.

Fun Fact Quiz

What game combines soccer with rocket-powered cars?

A. Fall Guys

B. Rocket League

C. Roblox

D. Beat Saber

Game
Create Your Own Puzzle

You've played lots of games, but now it's time to make your very own! Let's create a fun puzzle that you can challenge others to solve.

How to Play:

Step 1: Think about something cool you learned in this book. Can you create a word scramble, match-up game, or riddle about it?

Step 2: Write it down and show it to a friend or family member. Ask them to solve your puzzle.

Step 3: If they solve it, share something fun you learned from the chapter.

Tip: You can design puzzles related to each part or chapter of the book. You're now a game master!

Conclusion

So on the concluding note of this captivating tour through the written treasures of fact-filled curiosities, it is crucial to ponder upon the marvels witnessed and the truths unveiled. This book has guided you through vast and tremendous territories of exploration, from outer space to the fundamentals of the sea, from the times of dinosaurs to modern-day records of men and animals. Every chapter of this book has opened a new vista and kept alive the spirit of discovery that the world and the universe are a treasure trove of wonders. Our journey started with the existence and marvels of the universe while exploring the vastness of space and the surprising events that occur in other worlds.

The universe is limitless and its might is beyond human comprehension at the same time it contains many phenomena that are not even explained by science today. As for the exploration and discoveries from black holes and supernovas to the search for other life forms in space, the universe remains intriguing. Every piece of knowledge about the stars and planets puts the race closer to the complete picture of the universe but with the added realization of how much more there is yet to discover. Space is indeed the final frontier and as the technology continues to improve the following generations are likely to be witness to even more compelling discoveries. We then ventured into the diverse sphere of animals and their fascinating features and discoveries were made regarding the wonders of the animal kingdom that inhabits the earth.

From the chameleon, which is known to change colors as it seeks to hide from its predator to the speedy cheetah, people have always been amazed by animals' performance. Studying the peculiarities of animal activity and their ability to adapt to environmental conditions allows one to understand the richness of living creatures. Every creature, be it weird or peculiar, has a function in the orbits that support life in this world. The benefits of learning about different species are not limited to gaining facts but also developing a sense of appreciation towards living beings. Taking a brief look at the past, we went deep into the era of the dinosaurs, exploring the findings made to this day about these elusive beings. If there is one thing that can make any kid want to read more, it is a large dinosaur like the T. rex. However, understanding how these animals lived, evolved and then became extinct is beneficial in understanding the history of life on Earth. The fossils give an account of events that occurred before the existence of human beings and they provide society with another chapter of how the world developed. Through the lessons learned from dinosaurs, it becomes evident that nature acts in continual progression and morphs in manners that are yet to be fully comprehended.

The exploration of the human body made it clear that there are no greater marvels than ourselves. From the brain consisting of billions of cells to the heart and lungs, our bodies are full of awesome functions. Here we discovered some of the strangest facts about the human body, for instance, being able to swim without breathing for a few minutes and how our senses coordinate with one another. Hearing how the human body works can not only make one cherish their healthy body but also make one want to take care of their body. Just like all animals we have learned about, people also possess special attributes that help them to survive and it is always enjoyable and informative to learn about them.

During our trip, we also discovered major events in human history – early civilizations, and inventions that shaped the world. Man has always had their moments of creative thinking and courage and this has been depicted throughout the Histories that brought the modern society as we have it today. When Alexander Graham Bell developed the telephone by chance, or when the Wright brothers flew their first plane, such events helped them to realize that the world can be different due to innovation and the desire to move forward. This fight to learn about the past makes it possible to know the present while getting inspired by what the future holds. We also discovered the secrets of the sea or some of the most wondrous beings and locales within the depths thereof. Despite the fact that the ocean occupies over 70% of the Earth's surface, it is still one of the most unknown parts of our planet. Nevertheless, it hosts millions of species with many that are still unknown to science.

Some of the sea's biomes are rather sophisticated and sensitive, which makes me recall how significant it is to preserve this aspect of our planet. Indeed, as we progress with the discoveries we find deeper and deeper we are bound to discover even more about this life underwater. Starting with mythological stories all the way to contemporary records and achievements, we have seen how humans are capable of achieving the impossible. Whether in sports or technology, people are constantly striving for the next level, the next feat, the next step forward. Such stories of inspiring performance thus encourage all of us to strive and innovate in an effort to achieve similarly amazing feats. Want to know more? This book is more than just random facts…it is a means to encourage readers to keep on asking questions and seeking answers. Every piece of information that we have discussed today is an insignificant part of the vast world, and there is always more to learn. If your interests are in animals, space, history, or people's accomplishments, the world has many more wonders you can always discover.

Finally, let us gasp for more intriguing data to discover during this journey and encourage ourselves not to stop acquiring knowledge. The world is wonderful and amazing and there is so much out there that a person can come across. Therefore, do not stop asking questions and looking for knowledge, and above all – do not forget to have fun learning about the universe, the Earth, and everything else in between. As far as the fun is concerned, it is not over yet; it has only just started!

Printed in Great Britain
by Amazon